Praise for *Market Your Way to Growth*

"The world economic order has been reset, and the only way to survive is to grow continuously and sustainably. This book is a compelling road map to achieving growth based on first principles that businesses need to follow to negotiate a challenging yet promising future. The insights of Philip and Milton Kotler are incisive and perceptive, and they provide a blueprint for a successful enterprise—a must read."

—Mukesh D. Ambani, Chairman and Managing Director, Reliance Industries Limited, India

"Phil Kotler has done it again, giving us a superb distillation of the Big Issues of these difficult times and pragmatic advice on how companies can grow."

—Shumeet Banerji, CEO, Booz & Company

"I think that companies would benefit greatly if their senior management would read and discuss the eight ways to achieve growth in this difficult world economy. They would recognize pathways to growth that they have overlooked."

—Ram Charan, business consultant and author of
Execution: The Discipline of Getting Things Done
and other best-selling business books

"Phil Kotler is the reigning sage of marketing, with vast knowledge, penetrating insight, and a fabulous ability to synthesize a complex topic into truthful simplicity. A master teacher, Kotler continues to shape the minds of marketing leaders around the world—and through his writing, he can shape your mind, too."

—Jim Collins, author *Good to Great* and *Built to Last*

"*Market Your Way to Growth* goes way beyond marketing. It provides a fantastic framework for strategic leadership!"

—Marshall Goldsmith, executive coach and author of
New York Times best sellers *Mojo* and *What
Got You Here Won't Get You There*

"In this period of slow growth, this book is bound to stimulate new thoughts on strategy."

—Wen Bo He, President, China Bao Steel Corporation

"KMG China helped us to use these eight pathways to grow our civil aviation industrial park in Xian. We put customer demand before manufacturing start-up. We are now the largest general aviation air base in China."

—Qian Sheng Ji, CEO, China (Yanliang) National Aviation Hi-tech Industrial Base

"*Market Your Way to Growth: 8 Ways to Win* offers compelling insights for public companies that are operating in a rapidly changing and challenging global marketplace. The developed markets are slow, and emerging markets are on the fast track."

—William R. Johnson, Chairman, President, and CEO, H.J. Heinz Company

"Constant self-renewal is one of the essential traits for any business leader, and is an important theme in the Kotlers' book. Their wisdom, keen powers of observation, rich experience, and common sense will surely make this an important and practical business book."

—Robin Li, Co-Founder, Chairman and CEO of Baidu, Inc.

"In these uncertain times, growth is the single biggest challenge facing businesses across the world. The Kotler brothers have provided a comprehensive and valuable guide for businesses seeking fresh ways to grow."

—N. R. Narayana Murthy, Chairman Emeritus, Infosys, India

"The Kotler brothers are the masters of marketing and strategy! They can show you how to turn your marketing strategy into a growth strategy."

—Hermann Simon, Chairman of global consultancy Simon, Kucher & Partners and author of *Hidden Champions of the 21st Century*

"A brilliant guide for all business leaders seeking to move their companies to the fast lane, written by the greatest minds in strategic marketing."

—Prijono Sugiarto, CEO, Astra International, Indonesia

"Philip Kotler and Milton Kotler have given us many insightful suggestions and much help. Their theory is leading us to find new ways to grow in the global market."

—Xiu Guo Tang, Founder and CEO, SANY Group

"The eight pathways are a great place for a leadership team to start ideating about stepping up growth in what is likely a low-growth environment for the next decade."

—Peter F. Volanakis, Former President and COO, Corning Inc.

"Better marketing is vital for businesses in the era of social media and economic turbulence. I believe business leaders should all think strategically about marketing, as demonstrated in Philip and Milton Kotler's book."

—Shi Wang, Founder, Vanke Group

"The Kotler brothers have provided a pragmatic and holistic approach to delivering sustainable, profitable growth. They position the eight pathways and marketing as the strategic centerpoint of the transformation to higher growth."

—Katharyn M. White, Vice President Marketing,
IBM Global Business Services

"The Kotler brothers have made new contributions to growth strategy. Our company is actively practicing these eight strategies and becoming a major force in the global economy."

—Guang Quan Wu, CEO, China AVIC International

"Philip Kotler and Milton Kotler's book is a superb refresher course for managing and strategizing in a period of slow growth."

—Hang Xu, CEO, Mindray Group

"The Kotler brothers have made a fresh contribution to the literature on growth."

—Yuan Qing Yang, Chairman and CEO, Lenovo Group

"After *Marketing 3.0*, Philip Kotler is again leading the way to thinking about how to get out of the current slow growth period gripping today's companies and countries."

—Rui Min Zhang, Founder and CEO, Haier Group

MARKET
YOUR WAY TO GROWTH

WAYS TO WIN

PHILIP AND MILTON
KOTLER

WILEY

John Wiley & Sons, Inc.

From Philip:
To Nancy, my wife, my love, for your humor and
wisdom that I treasure.
To my international friends who gave me insight into the economies
of their countries: Evert Gummesson (Sweden), Pietro Guido (Italy),
Masatoshi Ito (Japan), Hermawan Kartajaya (Indonesia),
Fahim Kibria (World Marketing Summit), Kam Hon Lee (China),
Jose Salibi (Brazil), Hermann Simon (Germany),
and Walter Vieira (India).

From Milton:
To Greta Kotler, my partner in love, in family, in work and thought.
To Cao Hu, my steadfast colleague in building
Kotler Marketing in China.

CONTENTS

INTRODUCTION:
PREPARING TO MASTER THE EIGHT
PATHWAYS TO GROWTH

The years ahead will be best for those who learn to balance dreams and discipline. The future will belong to those who embrace the potential of wider opportunities but recognize the realities of more constrained resources, and find new solutions that permit doing more with less.

—Rosabeth Moss Kanter, 2011

We Live in a Two-Track World: Low/Slow Growth versus High/Fast Growth

Companies now find themselves operating in a two-track global economy. It is unlike the past economy—the one in the years before 2008. During that time, the world's countries typically all rose together and then dipped together as the global economy became increasingly interdependent. There is no doubt that the world today has countries operating at two different levels (low and high) and at two different speeds (slow and fast) relative to economic growth. At the time of this writing, both the United States and the European Union are facing the prospect of low and slow economic growth for the balance of this decade until the year 2020. Both will be marked by low growth rates—so low that their economies will not be able to create enough jobs to match the size and growth of their respective workforces—especially younger workers. They will also fail to keep pace with generating the tax revenues needed to even begin to deleverage their countries' enormous accumulated public debt, let alone bootstrap new industries. The U.S. economy may be unable to create enough jobs to match its population growth, which is expected to rise by almost 30 million from its current 2012 level of 313 million to 342 million by 2020.[1] Several EU countries are in, and some on the verge of, recession—and unemployment is acutely high.

Without substantial growth, unemployment rates could rise even higher than their current high rates, and more of each country's budget will be required to support the growing ranks of the unemployed. The costs of unemployment include lost growth, the price of unemployment benefits, health costs, and the general demoralization of the population.

Persons will remain unemployed for extended periods for *structural workforce* reasons (i.e., the advance of automation and a mismatch between open job positions requiring specific skills that the currently unemployed cannot fulfill), as well as *cyclical economic* reasons (i.e., reduced demand for currently unemployed skilled workers because of the downcycle, and the imposition of austerity measures that further reduce the number of jobs and incomes available for spending). [2]

The already swelled deficits in the United States and in Europe will then be financed in one of two ways. They will either print more money (i.e., *quantitative easing*), a potentially inflationary solution, especially at the very low interest rates currently in place and projected for the next several years. The alternative will be to raise taxes to levels that will dampen business investment and consumer spending.

Will the fragile state of the developed economies remain limited to them—or will their fragility spread to the stronger, faster-growing countries in the developing world?

The unfortunate answer is that the United States and Europe's lower growth is now shrinking developing world growth. China's growth rate fell from 10 percent to 8 percent, and the other BRIC countries (Brazil, Russia, and India) from 8 percent to 5 percent.[3] The higher growth rates in the Middle East and several African countries have come down; however, these economies are still in the fast lane compared to the United States (with a 2 percent growth rate) and the Eurozone (0.3 percent).

In the *very* slow lane are countries like Greece, Portugal, Italy, Ireland, and Spain—that are almost basket cases—as well as nations like Germany, France, and the United States that are struggling to squeeze out an annual growth rate of 1 to 3 percent. Although the BRIC countries are suffering from diminished growth as their exports fall in the low-growth countries, these countries' large populations make this a less dire issue. As their export revenues fall, BRIC countries can turn their attention to developing their domestic markets, which have not yet benefitted from the high growth rate. So Brazil, for example, can develop its northeast states, while China can develop in western regions. The fast-lane countries can stay alive and well by focusing their economic growth plans on their domestic market.

Business Responses in a Low-Growth Economy

Until the public sector decides what approach to take—either austerity or stimulus or some mix of these—it is impossible to predict the rate of economic recovery. Consumers and businesses are living under a cloud of uncertainty and keeping their purses closed tight—a scenario that only perpetuates low growth. There is even concern for further double dip recessions—and any economist who claims to be able to predict with certainty what the world economy will be like in the following years should clearly be ignored.

However, businesses have to act; they cannot wait for public policy to be enacted. So what options do companies have nowadays? There are two broad alternatives: cutting costs or restrategizing for growing revenues. Let's examine each of these in detail.

Cutting Costs. Many businesses that face declining demand will respond by using various methods to cut costs—for example, laying off some workers and trying to wrest more concessions from their suppliers. Of course, this leads their suppliers to cut their costs, lay off some workers, and wrest concessions from their own suppliers. This produces a cascade effect; the initial cuts from top businesses lead to further cuts all the way down the supply chain. The situation goes from bad to worse. And even though prices are falling as well as costs, customers hesitate to buy—because they expect to gain more by waiting for prices that might fall even further.

Restrategizing. It makes much more sense for each firm to restrategize rather than panic into cost cutting. Some firms believe the crisis to be an opportunity in disguise, and therefore "a terrible thing to waste." And in fact, an industry- or country-wide crisis *is* the best time to increase your market share. It is difficult in normal times for one company to gain share from other companies, because they are all well financed and fortified. But many firms become distressed during tougher times; they cannot get enough cash from their bank, or their cost of borrowing rises; they let go of some key employees; they are stuck with swollen inventories; and so on. This is the time that firms with sufficient cash can expand on the cheap; namely by acquiring good talent, purchasing inventories at distressed prices—perhaps even buying up competitors. For example, during the recent recession—while most air carriers were cutting their costs—Jet Blue planned to add 70 new planes and billions of dollars of new debt to continue its rapid growth. We will speak of Jet Blue later.

Restrategizing takes many forms; specifically, a company has to ask such questions as:

- Do we have any fat in our system? If so, let's cut it out (but be careful not to cut out any muscle).

- Are there certain market segments that will no longer be profitable? If so, let's move our money to more profitable segments.

- Are there some geographical areas that will no longer be profitable? If so, let's move our money to more profitable geographical areas.

- Are there some products and services that are losing money? If so, let's move our money to products and services that have more potential.

- Do we lose money by serving some customers? Let them buy from our competitors and bleed them rather than us.

- Are we taking advantage of low labor and capital cost sectors of our domestic and international economies to reduce cost and gain competitive price advantage?

Posing these and similar questions will allow a company to restrategize and take advantage of the crisis—instead of becoming another victim of it.

How should companies plan to grow—let alone prosper—in a low-growth economy? We are not looking for a prescription for raw growth, namely, growth at *any* cost. We all remember the businessman who prices his goods below his cost. "How are you going to make a profit?" He answers, "Volume." This is a Ponzi scheme—and it's not our answer. When we talk about *growth* as a company objective, we mean *profitable growth*—at least, that which is profitable in the long run, even if not in the short run. And we would add one more crucial adjective here: *sustainable* growth. By this, we mean helping the company's other partners to do well and helping the planet to thrive with clean air, water, and natural resources.

As such, our purpose in this book is to define the major pathways toward achieving profitable and sustainable growth.

The best way for a company to achieve steady growth is to have a clear company *purpose* and *goal*—and to ensure that all stakeholders are *passionate* about achieving the goal. Although this passion is manifest during a war period, it needs to be manifest during times of peace as well. The goal might be to become the best-performing economic engine in that particular industry. A hospital that wants to be one of the best hospitals in the world at treating illness will continue to learn from medical discoveries and from other hospitals' best practices. The earth-moving equipment company that wants to build new structures in the most efficient way possible will adopt the latest technology and learn from its best competitors.

Obviously, some companies will find clever short-term ways to make money in a crisis, and others still will have to survive by cutting their costs and prices. Unfortunately, cutting their costs include payroll cuts—thereby putting more persons in the unemployment line. Cutting prices means reducing profit margins, which leave these firms weaker—especially when facing strong competitors. Being weaker means that they are more likely to be acquired by their competitors at a cheap price or vanish through liquidation.

What Should Companies Do in a Low-Growth Economy?

Let's figure out how businesses can grow in a low-growth global economy and *prosper*—and for this, we will propose two things. The first is to recognize the nine megatrends that point out the major areas of opportunity. The second is to master the eight pathways that can deliver growth even in a slow growth economy.

Capitalizing on the Nine Megatrends

Here is our list of the nine megatrends that will affect growth and opportunity in the decade from 2013 to 2023:

1. Global redistribution of wealth and economic power.
2. Strategic refocusing from global to regional, regional to local.
3. Continued urbanization and growing infrastructure needs.
4. Growing number of opportunities arising out of science and technology.
5. Acceleration of the green global economy.
6. Rapidly changing social values.
7. Growing cooperation between private and public sectors.
8. Customer empowerment and the information revolution.
9. Hypercompetition and disruptive innovation.

The following is a thorough explanation of how any business can capitalize on each of these megatrends.

1. Global redistribution of wealth and economic power.

Since the 1500s, Western Europe has been the dominant economic power through the colonial global expansion of the British, Dutch, French, Spaniards, and Portuguese. The United States took the leadership in the nineteenth century—more through indigenous growth than colonization. The United States became the major world power from 1945 until recently—when talk about U.S. indebtedness and decline has been increasing. There is no doubt that economic power had initially shifted primarily to Japan and then the Middle East with their oil preeminence, more recently to the Asian tigers, and now primarily to China and India.

But it is also critical to note the growing concentration of wealth within most countries. Many of the new millionaires and billionaires are coming out of emerging countries. The good news is that some developing economies have high amounts of capital waiting to be utilized. There are now seven major sovereign funds with huge amounts of capital. Capital supply is not the problem. Major companies that need more capital can tap some of these sources of wealth. The problem is that the average citizen's purchasing power remains low—and therefore, spending remains low.

This megatrend is of special interest to luxury goods companies such as Louis Vuitton, BMW, Hermès, Gucci, Rolex, and others. These brands have opened outlets in countries where wealth is growing rapidly—China, Brazil, India, Russia, and Mexico, to name a few. In São Paulo, Brazil, the super-wealthy fly their helicopters to the roof of a major upscale department store where they park and then descend to do their shopping. The growth of the wealthy is leading luxury hotels such as Four Seasons to decide where to build their next properties. Private aircraft companies such as Gulf Stream and yacht makers are approaching the super-rich for plane and yacht sales. The lesson for your business is to consider growth opportunities for marketing to super-rich niches.

2. Strategic refocusing from global to regional, regional to local.

When opportunities are abundant, companies will move to the top-tier regional markets and cities. Chains like McDonald's and Starbucks have moved into Europe—first to major capital cities, and subsequently to second-tier cities. A major executive training firm called HSM Brazil—which had initially conducted its programs in São Paulo and Rio de Janeiro—is now taking its training programs to less well-known Brazilian cities such as Fortaleza, Porte Alegre, and Recife.

3. Continued urbanization and growing infrastructure needs.

Urbanization is highly likely to continue. Whereas major cities used to be under 10 million in size, cities today—including Shanghai, Beijing, Mumbai, São Paulo, Mexico City, and others—are approaching populations of 20 million. Furthermore, new cities continue to come into being. China itself is laying plans for the creation of many new cities and towns in part to absorb urbanization growth and to put brakes on further growth of the established megacities. As these cities grow, they require roads, electricity, energy, buildings, water sourcing, and sanitation facilities—all of which will produce jobs and require workers. Companies such as Caterpillar, General Electric, and Cemex are profiting by moving their products and services to established cities that are growing, as well as to new cities being built.

4. Growing number of opportunities arising out of science and technology.

There is no shortage of opportunities. The world is saddled with old problems that still need solutions—poverty,

water shortage, air and water pollution, and global warming,
to name a few. Businesses and consumers have many
functional and emotional desires they are eager to satisfy. And
then there are the rapidly emerging new sciences—life
sciences, personalized medicine, functional foods, new
energy, and nanotechnology—areas ready for refinement and
exploitation. High-tech companies such as Google, Facebook,
Apple, and Amazon have thrived by bringing their services
worldwide.

5. Acceleration of the green global economy.

Most of the world's businesses and citizens now recognize
the fragility of Mother Earth as exploitation of her resources
continues at an alarming rate—producing pollution and
scarcities in its wake. Aside from the world economy running
out of certain essential minerals, we have endangered our
natural resources. Forests are being cut down to burn wood
for cooking, and the evidence of overfishing is undeniable.
One of the collective nightmares haunting cities such as
Amsterdam, Venice, and New York is the possibility of
uncontrolled global warming—which would lead to rising sea
levels that could potentially drown these cities or cripple their
commerce. There is a growing need for regulation and
innovation to find ways to reduce energy use, contain
pollution, and recycle materials.

Resource scarcity and pollution provide numerous
opportunities for businesses. General Electric CEO Jeffrey
Immelt launched a program called Ecomagination to show
how money could be made by solving challenging global
problems. GE ventured into the solar panel and wind turbine
businesses to generate other sources of energy. Similarly, retail
chain Walmart is replacing its gas-guzzling trucks with
fuel-efficient vehicles that use 50 percent less fuel. Automobile

companies are moving more swiftly into hybrid and pure electric cars and trucks. Resource companies are moving into fracking and finding new reserves of natural gas. What is *your* company doing to help save the planet by going green?

6. Rapidly changing social values.

The digital revolution has led to an explosion of information and communication contents and channels. I can get an answer to almost any question within a matter of seconds by searching on Google—a website that people have described as closest to God in being all-knowing. I can reach 600 friends from all over the world on Facebook and communicate with them instantly through e-mail, headsets, or Skype. I can watch videos from around the world to see different cultures in action. New ideas, fads, and fashions spread faster than ever—a trend that makes all of us more aware of other beliefs, norms, mores, and practices, while throwing our own ways into sharper relief.

We are far from being a homogeneous society. There are so many different "tribes" with which citizens can identify. In their book *Microtrends*, authors Mark Penn and Kinney Zalesne describe 75 micro groups that have particular needs and wants that alert businesses should recognize as opportunities.[4] Consider just the following seven: single-woman households, women marrying young men, the working retired, stay-at-home workers, office romancers, Protestant Hispanics, and extreme commuters. Each group will have a specific set of needs and wants. Take, for example, the increasing number of stay-at-home workers. They need an office or some kind of working space somewhere in the house, stationery supplies, telecommunication equipment, and other things that marketing research with this group would reveal.

Each microtrend group represents a possible growth opportunity.

In fact, this phenomenon has led author Greg Verdino to propose an entirely new method for serving microgroups. In his 2010 book, *Micromarketing: Get Big Results by Thinking and Acting Small*, Verdino shows how small entrepreneurs can use the power of viral marketing to reach and sell to these groups.[5] His idea is to recruit social networking folks (called *micromavens*) who will use viral marketing to spread word of mouth about existing or new products and services. Yelp has had outstanding success in rating local restaurants, shops and services. Groupon, a sales promotion company, micro-markets local restaurant and service deals to local consumers.

7. Growing cooperation between private and public sectors.

Much time has been spent—and wasted—in battles between the advocates of private enterprise and those who defend government activities and investments. The first group would limit government to spending money on national defense, public safety, and some physical and social infrastructure development. The second group sees the need for government to make broader investments in physical infrastructure, industrial stimulus, as well as the social infrastructure of health, education, welfare, and social and cultural advancement. Whatever one's opinion, the fact is that we need more partnership and less venom between the two groups. Government in most of the West is not attempting to socialize businesses and run them: the Soviet experiment exposed the inherent disasters of government running everything. Yet partnerships between local governments and local private enterprise, as well as state government and private enterprise, can do a great deal to advance local and state economic development. And we are seeing more evidence of successful partnering nowadays.

8. Customer empowerment and the information revolution.

The digital revolution has caused a tremendous shift in the power relations between sellers, middlemen, and buyers. In the predigital days, sellers enjoyed a monopoly on the information that would go to consumers about the seller's products and services. We basically learned about a company through its ads and what stock analysts would say about it. Buyers had a lot of choices of competitors, but very limited information about each. A few would rely on Consumer Reports and family opinions, but most remained largely uninformed.

Today, hardly anyone buys a new car without first getting on the Internet and clicking on an automobile website, clicking on Facebook and collecting their friend's impressions and experiences, going on Edmunds.com to read opinions not only about the car but what the real price should be, and going to J.D. Power and Associates to see how satisfied recent car buyers were with their car choice. The customer is empowered; the Customer is truly King. And he and she are as well-informed as the sellers. Information between buyers and sellers is now symmetric rather than asymmetric. Eventually, it will reach a point where low-quality companies will die quicker. When consumers are able to easily and quickly ascertain the level of a seller's products and service, poor-performing companies will enter the business graveyard quicker. Long-lasting companies will be those that absolutely understand their target market's needs and wants and do a superior job of satisfying them.

9. Hypercompetition and disruptive innovation.

The digital revolution has not only made the Customer the King; it has also disrupted and destroyed many businesses that could be better run digitally without market intermediaries. We can get our music without going to a music store; we can download a book without visiting a bookstore; we can make our own travel arrangements without a travel agent; and we don't need the newspaper delivered anymore: iTunes for music, Kindle for ebooks, Travelocity for travel, and both the *Wall Street Journal* and the *Financial Times* offer online-only subscription options. Almost every business needs to consider reinventing itself in digital terms. Just as Kodak went bankrupt when digital cameras did away with the need for film, and store-based retailing is losing business to online retailing, *every* business needs to adapt and innovate. Existing companies need not only track their immediate competitors, but pay equal attention to competitors who might emerge from a garage with an exciting new product or a business model—one that delivers lower prices and enhanced quality and convenience.

The Eight Pathways to Sustainable Growth

Now we can turn our attention to the eight most promising pathways to growth. Even when a business is stuck in a low or slowing high-growth economy, it can benefit from exploring these. We would name the study of these eight pathways *growth economics*. However, let us be clear on one thing: growth *in itself* is not a sufficient goal. There are many ways for a business to grow. It can grow by aggressively cutting its prices and sustain large losses. It can grow in spurts, rather than systematically and continuously. We often distinguish between unmanaged growth and managed growth.

Our interest lies in achieving growth that is (1) profitable and (2) sustainable. And *profitable* means not only in the short run but in the long run as well. Sometimes a company has to invest deeply and bear lower profits for the sake of producing higher profits in the long run. By sustainable, we mean that in the long run a company meets both its stakeholderss' interests and those of the community and society at large. A business that grows rapidly but leaves behind air, water, and land pollution is not sustaining the earth's natural resources—something that will eventually hurt *all* businesses.

Our interest is to examine the eight pathways and pose questions at the end of each that each company should answer to determine whether it is making the best use of that pathway to achieve profitable and sustainable growth. Each pathway has been described dozens of times. There are many detailed books on how to manage successful mergers and acquisitions, build stronger brands, develop a more innovative culture, and seek opportunities by going abroad—as well as all the others. The problem occurs when a company feels that it can win big by proceeding along just one pathway—when in truth, it may take several to succeed.

We wrote this book to assemble the eight pathways in one place, and enable motivated businesses to take a broader view of where they stand in relation to the opportunities present in all eight. Here is what your company might find in assessing its standing on the eight pathways:

- In the best case, your company has mastered all eight pathways—which explains your high sales and profit growth.

- Or you learn that your company has mastered a few of the pathways and is sorely deficient in the others. Your task is to concentrate on improving your skills in the deficient pathways by developing and following a real, actionable plan.

- Or you might learn that your company is quite average in most of these pathways in comparison to your strongest competitors. You will have to figure which pathways to strengthen first to give the best early results as you work from

being an average-performing company to a
superior-performing company.

Now we are ready to ask: What are the eight pathways that
companies need to master to achieve profitable and sustainable
growth? The pathways will be described in the eight chapters of
this book and come out of answering the following questions:

1. Grow by Building Your Market Share. What is the best way to
   outperform your competitors and grow your market share?
   (Chapter 1)

2. Grow through Developing Committed Customers and
   Stakeholders. How can your company create fans and develop
   dedicated value chain partners? (Chapter 2)

3. Grow by Developing a Powerful Brand. What can your
   company do to design and implement a powerful brand to
   serve as a living platform for its strategy and actions?
   (Chapter 3)

4. Grow by Innovating New Products, Services, and Experiences.
   How can your company develop a culture of innovation and
   create fresh new offerings and experiences? (Chapter 4)

5. Grow by International Expansion. How can you successfully
   identify and enter international macro and micro pockets of
   high growth? (Chapter 5)

6. Grow by Mergers, Acquisitions, Alliances, and Joint Ventures.
   How can your company grow through identifying attractive
   partnering opportunities through mergers, acquisitions,
   alliances, and joint ventures? (Chapter 6)

7. Grow by Building an Outstanding Reputation for Social
   Responsibility. How can your company improve its social
   character to win more respect and support from the public
   and its stakeholders? (Chapter 7)

8. Grow by Partnering with Government and NGOs. How can your company find opportunities to work with government and NGOs to meet public, social, and private needs better? (Chapter 8)

Our thesis is that Strategic Marketing thinking plays a major role in all eight pathways. Marketing is the force that centers on the Customer, who is the key to Consumption, Spending, and Job Creation. Marketing is the New Economics that proposes tangible actions that can create and increase economic competition and innovation within and between nations.

By using these pathways, your company will be able to restrategize and find opportunities for growth in a distressed economy.

Conclusion

The financial meltdown and the lingering crises plaguing the global economy require an intelligent response from public policy makers—as well as from individual firms. Will it be austerity or stimulus from the public sector? Will it be cost and price cutting or restrategizing from private business?

Our task in each of the following eight chapters is to focus on what private businesses can do to invest and spend intelligently, even in the face of high political uncertainty and a rapidly changing economic environment. We hope to show how companies can use the eight pathways of growth to achieve long-term sustainable growth and prosperity.

Questions

1. In which of the eight pathways is your company strongest? Weakest?

2. If you could strengthen your standing on one of the eight pathways, which would it be? Why?

3. Considering the list of nine megatrends, which megatrend would you suggest focusing on now as the best opportunity area for your company?

4. Which would have a better impact on your company's performance: (1) the nation pushes austerity, or (2) the nation pushes stimulus? Explain why.

1 Grow by Building Your Market Share

Poor firms ignore their competitors; average firms copy their competitors; winning firms lead their competitors.

In a recent survey, the Conference Board asked CEOs to rank various business priorities and found unsurprisingly, that the top priority was business growth. Procter & Gamble (P&G) CEO Bob McDonald highlighted the point by saying "We've got to grow; that's the main thing."[1] Growth is the goal in normal times, and is especially the goal in depressed times.

Growth, however, is not that easy to achieve, even in normal times. And even before the Great Recession started in 2008, times were far from normal. Excess supply existed in almost every industry. Companies found it hard to raise or even hold prices. Their margins were low and in danger of getting lower.

The onset of recession and its slow recovery have only worsened the situation. Companies find that they don't merely need a growth strategy; they need a *defense* strategy. However, they're far more lax about defense than about growth—since growth is where the action is and where the rewards go. CEOs don't get kudos for keeping what they have in place; they get kudos for expanding it.[2] Yet in hard times, the attacks on one's core business will increase in frequency and severity as a result of competitors' desperation. Since many companies are losing customers or sales, they are willing to cut prices and resort to aggressive or predatory moves against other competitors to preserve these sales. And because their customers are having problems too, their customers are likely to press for deeper discounts.

Companies will usually turn to many traditional strategies—such as cost reduction, product and package adaptation, and new communication tactics—to preserve their margins. But today's companies are facing even more challenges than before: cheaper competition from abroad, quick competitive reaction, price transparency, and lost control over messages that customers receive.

A company has three options with respect to handling competitors who cut their prices:

1. Keep prices where they are, but add other benefits.

2. Give discounts to those worthwhile customers who press for a deeper discount.

3. Lower the prices for all customers.

Companies can hope to maintain their current prices by augmenting their benefit package. They can improve product features, offer better delivery terms, or improve their service quality. But if they can't create an augmented benefit package, they will have to reduce their prices directly or through sales promotion tactics (discounts, rebates, and so on). To preserve their profit margin, they would have to trim their costs.

As such, we urge businesses to take the following five steps to develop plans for gaining market share:

1. Search for more efficiency.

2. Prepare an analysis of Strengths, Weaknesses, Opportunities, and Threats (SWOT).

3. Improve your financial and marketing strength.

4. Reassess your marketing mix and profile.

5. Develop winning market share strategies.

Let's look at each in detail.

Search for More Efficiency

Every business will develop "fat" in normal good times, since companies are more generous and spend more liberally during periods of growth. There is less financial and operational discipline. Profits grow, but fat accumulates. In fact, we could probably find 15 to 20 percent fat in a company during good times.

Even a major company will eventually recognize that its costs have become too high and that it needs to cut them. For example, when P&G's business growth slowed down some years ago, the company recognized that its marketing costs were 25 percent of sales—and that they needed to reduce them to 20 percent of its sales. As such, P&G took the following steps:

- Reduced the number of its sizes and versions of its various products, including toothpaste, detergents, soaps, and so on.

- Standardized more of its product, packaging, and advertising formulations to reduce costs.

- Dropped some of its weaker brands (i.e., eliminating two from the eight brands of detergents that they'd carried).

- Reduced investment in new product development and only concentrated on the most promising concepts.

Clearly, every company facing a period of prolonged low economic growth has to take steps to become leaner. Exhibit 1.1 lists questions that your company should consider.

Exhibit 1.1 Searching for Ways to Bring Down Costs

Can our company . . .

- Lower the costs of paper, packaging, and other inputs by negotiating for lower prices or switching to lower-cost suppliers?

- Switch to lower-cost transportation carriers?

- Close down sales offices that aren't getting much use—and have more sales people who can work out of their home as a result of home-based information and communication resources?

- Put our advertising agency on a pay-for-performance basis? (Procter & Gamble has put most of its advertising agency on this pay basis.)

- Replace higher-cost traditional communication channels with lower-cost digital channels?

- Achieve more impact by shifting some promotion money from 30-second TV commercials into public relations and new social media?

- Drop some product features or services to which customers don't seem to assign much value?

- Hold fewer or shorter staff meetings in lower-cost locations, and/or hold these meetings via audio, video, or web teleconferencing (Cisco, a prime teleconferencing supplier, advertises "Meet Face-to-Face Without Travel").

Prepare a SWOT Analysis

Every company needs to prepare a fresh SWOT analysis—Strengths, Weaknesses, Opportunities, Threats—to reassess its current situation. You want to size up each SWOT element not only in absolute terms but in relation to key competitors. So even if your company maintains its quality at 95 percent, it's not an advantage if your key competitor maintains its quality at 98 percent—and customers prefer 98 percent quality.

Let's first look at your company's strengths and weaknesses and then examine your opportunities and threats.

Strengths and Weaknesses. Every business has a set of capabilities. Any capability that is an important contributor to the company's performance can be at one of four levels: superior, good, average, or poor in relation to competitors. If that capability is superior or good, we will call it a Strength—and we hope that the company uses it competitively. If that capability is poor, then it is clearly a Weakness. But whether it makes a great difference depends on how much that capability contributes to company performance. For example—T-Mobile's transmission network in the United States was a weakness and led the company to seek a merger with AT&T. This is an example of a weakness that has high relevance to company performance.

Exhibit 1.2 shows a list of strengths and weaknesses in four major company areas that will help the company to make a strength and weaknesses assessment.

Exhibit 1.2 Strengths/Weaknesses Analysis

	Performance			Importance		
	Hi	Med	Low	Hi	Med	Low
Marketing						
1. Company reputation						
2. Market share						
3. Customer satisfaction						
4. Customer retention						
5. Product quality						
6. Service quality						
7. Pricing effectiveness						
8. Distribution effectiveness						
9. Promotion effectiveness						
10. Sales force effectiveness						
11. Innovation effectiveness						
12. Geographical coverage						
Finance						
13. Capital cost or availability						
14. Cash flow						
15. Financial stability						

	Performance			Importance		
	Hi	Med	Low	Hi	Med	Low
Manufacturing						
16. Facilities						
17. Economies of scale						
18. Capacity						
19. Able, dedicated workforce						
20. Ability to produce on time						
21. Manufacturing skill						
Organization						
22. Visionary/capable leadership						
23. Dedicated employees						
24. Entrepreneurial orientation						
25. Flexible or responsive						

The company will learn two important things from this exercise: First, it will be able to identify its major strengths. But perhaps more importantly, it will also be able to discern that some of these strengths don't really matter much to customers. Secondly, it will know its major weaknesses—and determine which weaknesses are not of much consequence to the buyers. It should keep its eyes on those strengths that have the most importance to the customers and to running its type of business successfully.

Opportunities and Threats. The next step is to take a more dynamic view of external and emerging factors that can affect a company's performance. There are two tools—Early Warning

Systems and Scenario Planning—that are helpful in detecting opportunities and threats.

Early Warning Systems. We are living in an age of global interconnectedness where events taking place in one part of the world can have a profound effect in other parts of the world. For example, the March 11, 2011, Japanese earthquake killed hundreds of Japanese and damaged supplies and production and sales. It kept everyone on edge for months as to whether the nearby damaged nuclear plant would leak radiation into the atmosphere. Japanese companies and their customers lost a great deal of sales.

Change is occurring at increasing speed and disrupting the behavior of customers, suppliers, distributors, products, and services. Any company might suddenly find its relationships and productivity collapsing as a result of disruptive events, technology, or innovation. Just consider how the digital revolution has dampened or destroyed music stores, bookstores, and newspapers. And it isn't just catastrophic or global events that can have this effect; one or two persons working in a small garage might invent something that changes the nature of a whole industry or society. Consider the early case of Bill Hewlett and Dave Packard who started Hewlett-Packard, and more recently individuals like Bill Gates (Microsoft), Steve Jobs (Apple), Mark Zuckerberg (Facebook), and Larry Page and Sergey Brin (Google).

To promote knowledge of emerging opportunities and threats, companies must assign monitoring responsibilities for different components of its environment to various staff members. Exhibit 1.3 provides a guide for the components that they need to watch. For example, you'd want to assign one staff person to each competitor, so that you can gather as much information as possible about that competitor. This way, if the company's salesperson is bidding against a specific competitor, the salesperson could contact the company's knowledge expert and find out what that competitor is likely to do in its bidding strategy. If the company does not build up a team of internal experts, it will have to get this information by working with a business intelligence firm.

Exhibit 1.3 Components of an Early Warning System

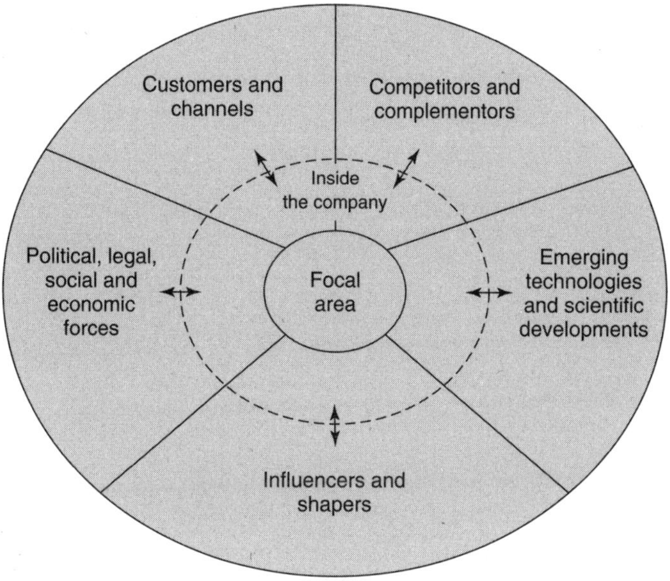

Source: George S. Day and Paul J.H. Shoemaker, *Peripheral Vision* (Boston: Harvard Business School Press, 2006).

Being a knowledge expert on some component need not be a full-time job; it's simply an added responsibility. Companies must assign specific responsibilities, however, since we can't expect everyone in the company to be observing *everything*.

An Early Warning System allows you to turn some of these findings into opportunities. For example, someone from your company might uncover that a major competitor is planning to close one its plants—which is an opportunity for your company to buy their business or at least grab market share.

Some findings that you unearth will be threats. Vonage, for example, was an early pioneer in the selling of substantially lower cost telecommunications packages for companies, including a plan for unlimited international calling to more than 60 countries for a flat monthly rate. Now it must respond to the news that Microsoft has acquired Skype and will be a prime competitor to Vonage.

You need to estimate both the seriousness and probability for every threat or opportunity. You can discount certain matters whose impact is not very serious or whose likelihood is not very probable.

The next step is to put together the overall picture of opportunities and threats—which you can do by utilizing the second tool: scenario planning. Scenario planning was developed initially for military planning where there is a high degree of uncertainty. Among the early company users was Royal Dutch/Shell which had to make huge investments without knowing how many oil fields would be found, how much demand for oil would exist, and the impact of the environmental movement on oil demand. Pfizer has been a big user of scenario planning in dealing with the uncertainties of drug price regulation and the new health care legislation (Obama plan).

Scenario planning involves the company in setting up different scenarios of what might happen to key variables affecting the company. The company can generate many scenarios but it is best to limit the number. Suppose the company develops three scenarios:

1. A normal one resembling the present.
2. A pessimistic scenario in which the threats outnumber the opportunities.

3. An optimistic scenario in which the opportunities outnumber the threats.

Exhibit 1.4 diagrams a case of three scenarios.

Exhibit 1.4 Viewing Three Different Scenarios

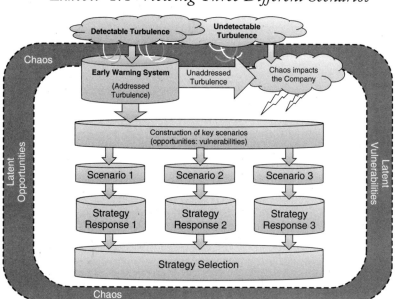

Source: Philip Kotler and John A. Caslione, *Chaotics: The Business of Managing and Marketing in the Age of Turbulence* (New York: AMACOM, 2009).

The company's senior staff reviews possible economic, social, technical, and political environments in which the company might operate in the coming period. One scenario might view the environment to be the same as the present one. Another scenario might take a pessimistic view and assume the worst. A third scenario might take an optimistic view and assume the best.

The value of building scenarios is not that it will be easy to predict their probability; in fact, it is hard to predict the likelihood of any of the three scenarios. But the aim of scenario building is to stretch our imagination about what could potentially happen because we might get some new ideas or determine in advance how to respond if any of these scenarios occurred. The idea is to use scenario planning as a way to think out of the box and broaden our perspective of the surrounding eco-system and its various possibilities and patterns. The company should prepare contingency plans for the most serious threats.

Companies can use other tools as well to cope with the heightened uncertainty. *Monte Carlo simulation* is used by such companies as Eli Lilly, Sears, General Motors, and Procter and Gamble to develop a probability distribution that shows the frequency of different outcomes using a stated strategy. *War gaming*, another tool, has been used by Merck and Company to learn how different players might react to a major change that is initiated by one of the players and the ensuing actions and reactions. Companies also use *decision trees* to enumerate a sequence of possible decisions and likely outcomes that might result.

Improve Your Financial and Marketing Strength

When a firm considers its options in the face of a low growth economic picture, its strategy options depend heavily on the level of its strength in finance and in marketing. According to global management and strategy consulting firm Booz & Company, we can distinguish four company situations. As displayed in Exhibit 1.5, the firm's best strategy is different in each situation.

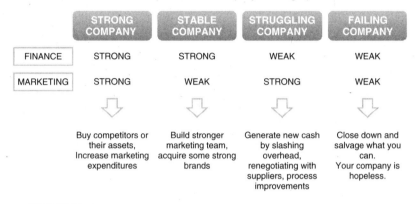

Exhibit 1.5 What Type of Company Are You?

It depends on the company's strategic profile

	STRONG COMPANY	STABLE COMPANY	STRUGGLING COMPANY	FAILING COMPANY
FINANCE	STRONG	STRONG	WEAK	WEAK
MARKETING	STRONG	WEAK	STRONG	WEAK
	⇩	⇩	⇩	⇩
	Buy competitors or their assets, Increase marketing expenditures	Build stronger marketing team, acquire some strong brands	Generate new cash by slashing overhead, renegotiating with suppliers, process improvements	Close down and salvage what you can. Your company is hopeless.

Source: Booz & Company.

1. **Strong company.** This business is endowed with very good financial and marketing capability. It has talented marketing managers and a lot of money available. In this case, the firm should be an aggressor and press to increase its market share. It should augment marketing campaigning and consider buying one or more weak competitors or their assets, as well as going after financially strapped competitors. Some competitors will sell some of their assets or even their whole business. This is a golden time for a firm like Google that is blessed with both strong finance and marketing.

2. **Stable company**. This business is strong financially, with money to spend, but lacks the marketing skills to capitalize on its opportunities. In some ways, Microsoft fits this picture in having lots of money but not finding it easy to grow. It needs to use its funds to attract marketing talent and build a stronger

team. It might well be that weakening competitors have laid off some expert marketers who are looking for a company where they can apply their marketing skills. This business should also consider buying some strong brands rather than trying to build new ones from scratch. If this company can ratchet up its marketing capability, it will become more like the first business: one strong in both finance and marketing.

3. **Struggling company**. A third business can be strong in marketing, waiting to implement many ideas—but lacking in sufficient funds to carry them out. Chrysler has an innovative history but at the present it needs more funds to grow. It can try to generate additional cash by slashing overhead, renegotiating with suppliers, and improving its processes. This firm needs to apply its strong marketing know-how to convince bankers and other money sources to lend funds to them. If this company succeeds in getting capital to improve its financial strength, it will have financial and marketing strength and therefore be like firm number one—ready to wrest share from its competitors.

4. **Failing company**. A fourth kind of business may lack both finance and marketing skills. We cannot offer this firm any hope to prosper, let alone survive, in a recessed or low growth economy. This may characterize JCPenney today, which needs to either find a new strategy or sell out to some other investor.

Reassess and Improve Your Marketing Mix and Market Profile

During a market slowdown, companies start desperately searching for ways to reduce their costs. They usually select three departments for quick cost cutting: new product development, human resources, and marketing. Specifically, they put new products on hold; human resources stops spending money on recruitment and training; and marketing is curtailed in less critical markets.

Let's focus on marketing here, since there is a lot of misunderstanding about best marketing practices during a recession. The general perception is that many companies will reduce their TV advertising. They believe that while TV advertising can help build the brand in the long run, they desperately need to cut costs *today*. They might also consider dropping some products, services, market segments, and even particular customers who cost more than they are worth.

However, instead of assuming that all companies struggling with money should simply cut their marketing budgets, let's review the findings of a recent 2011 Kotler Marketing Group Research Report called *Marketing through Difficult Times: Best Practices of Companies that Found Ways to Prosper During the Great Recession*. Here are the findings:[3]

General Findings

- The majority of CMOs said their companies maintained or even increased resource allocation to a set of core marketing activities. These companies emphasized product line profitability and expanded online marketing and strategic account management efforts.

- Online and digital marketing efforts continued to grow in importance during the Great Recession. Indeed, because such tools are often relatively inexpensive, our current economic situation seems to have encouraged firms to invest in them.

- The continued emphasis on marketing activities (including online and digital marketing) was accompanied by significant reductions in marketing personnel. In short, firms have sought to do more with less.

- This doing-more-with-less approach has been coupled with a relative privileging of efforts that promise short-term payoffs and have a clear and direct impact on the bottom line. Though understandable in light of economic circumstances, this development raises concerns about the long-term sustainability and effectiveness of firms' commitment to marketing.

The researchers looked more closely at firms' performances in their study, and then classified them into two groups: High-Performing vs. Low-Performing Firms. They asked each firm to rate its sales growth relative to its industry. Those reporting that their sales growth exceeded the industry average were called high-performing firms; the others were classified as low-performing firms. The researchers then looked up public records of 50 of the companies in their sample, comparing their actual change in sales to relevant industry averages, and found the self-reported data to be reliable with no significant bias. Here are two significant differences between the high-performing and low-performing firms:

1. Though both high- and low-performing firms exhibited a continuing commitment to marketing during the Great Recession, high-performing firms were distinguished by a *greater level of commitment*.
2. High-performing firms had a *stronger marketing culture* than low-performing firms.

Time to Reassess Your Marketing Strategy

Let's turn now to the question of what your company should do during the onset of a recession. You certainly need to reassess your market segments and customers; your products and services; and your promotion mix. Let's examine each of these steps individually.

Reassess Your Market Segments and Customers   Most
companies would like to sell their products and services to
everyone who buys in the product category. However, they
understand that the customers vary in what they want, value, and
can pay. Therefore, companies need to determine the
characteristics of the most suitable customers that they should
target. They need to sort the buyers into significant segments. You
can categorize customers in consumer markets by differences in
age, gender, income, education, or lifestyle, or some combination
of the above. The company is basically looking for a fairly
homogeneous group of customers and prospects who are similar
in their wants, buying criteria, and buying behavior. When the
company identifies a segment that it wants to serve—and *can*
serve in a superior fashion—it can describe this group to its
advertising agency and to its sales force. Then, the advertising and
sales people can choose efficient media and aim their messages to
hit the hot button that gets those customers and prospects to buy.

Here are some other considerations in segment thinking and
planning:

- A company need *not limit itself to one segment*. It may pursue
  a number of segments; however, each segment requires a
  tailored planning of product, price, place, and promotion.
  McDonald's, for example, has created separate marketing
  plans to attract mothers and children, teenagers, senior
  citizens, and different ethnic groups to its premises.

- A segment's *size and desires can change over time*. Therefore,
  companies must keep freshening their approach to each
  segment. Some segments will get smaller because of changing
  tastes or economic hardship. Persons who were happy with
  the company's brand may switch to a cheaper brand. In this
  case, a company should consider introducing a cheaper,
  second brand rather than lowering the price of its top brand.

The apparel maker Gap began to lose customers to cheaper brands. It took its less expensive chain operation called the Gap Warehouse and renamed it Old Navy, which today has more than 1,000 stores in the U.S. and Canada.

- The company needs to measure *each segment's profitability*, and will likely want to switch from serving a low-profit segment to a fast-growing, higher-profit segment. This will require a new 4-P plan for entering and prospering in this new segment. Hewlett-Packard has talked about possibly selling its slow growth PC division and focusing on the fast growing tablet market pioneered by Apple Computer. Its first venture in tablets was not successful but it will try again.

- Besides knowing the profitability or rate of return on serving each segment, the company can also benefit from estimating *the profitability of each customer* in the segment. It's apt to find that it's losing money on some customers who either buy too little or cost too much to serve. Most companies try to grade their customers in an effort to make these distinctions. A related development is that EBureau, a predictive analytics company, is able to assign scores from 0 to 99 indicating the buying power of individual customers. The buying power takes into account the person's occupation, home value, salary, and spending patterns. Clients buy these EScores to determine which of their "leads" should receive an offer. Companies will make offers to high e-score consumers and not bother to waste time and money pursuing low e-score consumers.

- Keep in mind, however, that customer profitability is only a *current* measure of the customer's value. It is therefore *better to estimate the customer's lifetime value*—something that will differ from one customer to the next. The estimate calls for projecting how many years customers are likely to remain customers, how much they are likely to buy, and the profit that the company will earn from them each year. The company then estimates the present value of the future income *stream from those customers*. A company wants to go all out when serving those customers who have high customer lifetime value.

- Although we described a segment as consisting of homogenous customers, we recognize that *some products attract very different customers*. For instance, motorcycle maker Harley Davidson Company has built a whole community of fans—including "tough guys," "professionals (lawyers, doctors)," women and others—all of whom love the company. Apple has also built a community of enthusiasts who differ in many ways—except for the fact that they love Apple. During a recession, a company that serves several subsegments must assess which of them to focus on—and which they can let go if it simply costs too much to serve and keep them happy.

Reassess Your Current Products and Services Most products, services, and brands are likely to exhibit life cycle characteristics. They appear at a certain point in time, grow popular if they meet a need, reach a plateau characterized as maturity, and then begin a decline. The length of each stage varies greatly, and sometimes a company or a market development gives the product a second life. For example, the product "nylon" has had several lives; it was successively incorporated in parachutes, women's hosiery, marine sails, clothing, and rubber tires. Many products, however, grow old and obsolete, and are replaced by newcomers. Company brands often have a longer life than product brands—which has been the case with machinery manufacturer Caterpillar or car maker Mercedes—despite the fact that many different products and product brands have passed through these companies and vanished.

The current product mix found in any company is likely to consist of yesterday's breadwinners, today's winners, and tomorrow's expected performers. A company needs to establish a system whereby it can monitor and evaluate the products in its line to determine which should receive increased or decreased support—and which should be eliminated. Philip Kotler proposed such a system in a *Harvard Business Review* article on "Phasing Out Weak Products."[4]

During a period of economic decline, every company has to take a hard look at the current and future position of its various products. This is the time to start flushing out the losers and increasing the support given to the winners. Consider a company such as Nike with so many lines of shoes. Some shoes will exhibit a sharp decline either because of fashion change or price. When this happens, production needs to be curtailed. If the decline is very serious, that line can be dropped and delisted.

Although we've talked most about products, services also require attention. During good times, a company can be generous in its provision of services by giving refunds, repairing products, sending holiday greetings, sponsoring member events, and the like. However, when times get tight, companies need to reconsider which services are important to customers, and which services would not be missed if dropped. This might compel a company to decide to make some services not free, but optional at a price.

Reassess Your Promotion Mix   During good times, companies are comfortable spending on advertising and other marketing activities because their competitors are doing this and the company wants to maintain a decent share of voice. They're aware that much advertising spending is an act of faith or insurance, rather than having an easily measured rate of Return on Marketing Investment (ROMI). But once an economic decline sets in, the company will start retrenching on promotion or shift from expensive to less-expensive promotion. It is easier for the company to see an actual penny saved than a hypothetical penny earned.

Members of the marketing department will be hard pressed to defend the existing budget. In some cases, they might even argue that this is the time to *increase* marketing expenditures—especially if all the competitors have slashed their marketing budgets. In normal times, a company can barely increase its market share; during an economic decline, it will be easier for strong companies to capture some share. But most company leaders prefer to reduce the marketing budget based on the assumption that marketing cannot do much in the short term to energize customer buying.

A downturn in business leads companies to rethink not only the size of their ad budget but also their mix of promotional tools. Some companies shift some TV money to radio or newspapers, especially when running sales promotions. Many companies have increased their social media expenditures, and others have increased their use of public relations and events spending. The big effort will go towards increasing sales promotion—discounts, rebates, two for the price of one, and so on—all of which are aimed to reduce the price in an effort to hold onto price-sensitive customers. But the company has to be aware that heavy sales promotion can detract from their image of being "better and different."

Although we have illustrated how to adapt the marketing mix during recession mainly for business-to-consumer (B2C) companies, much of this applies to business-to-business (B2B) companies as well—since these companies have few customers and are highly specialized. They have to assess their segments, individual customers, product mix, distribution mix, and promotion mix. Each customer is likely to want to renegotiate prices, seek fewer equipment features and less expensive models, and want more trade promotion support. Basically, your company has to decide which customers, segments, and product lines are worth keeping in the long run.

Market Share–Winning Strategies

Having looked at how a company can become trim and fit in general—and particularly, during a period of economic decline—we now turn to how the company can be precise in grabbing market share from its competitors.

The problem facing companies today is that there are too many fishermen and not enough fish in the market. It's a matter of eat lunch or be lunch—or, as stated by Gregory Rawlins, "If you're not part of the steamroller, you're a part of the road."

The first task is to identify your competitors. According to ancient philosopher Sun Tzu, "Time spent in reconnaissance is seldom wasted." Pay attention to those competitors who are going after your market with pretty much the same marketing mix. If their marketing budget is substantially larger than yours, you might consider going after a different market segment. If their marketing budget is substantially lower than yours, you may go for the kill. Elizabeth Arden could not keep up with competitors' like Estée Lauder and L'Oréal.

Companies often make this choice by determining which competitors are not doing a good job for their customers. This may be due to incompetence or the fact that the competitor has much more invested in another part of its enterprise—therefore causing this market to fail to receive its primary attention and funding. This would be exactly the kind of competitor to go after—because the parent company may decide to evacuate this market just as that competitor is being pounded and wounded. However, this is less likely to take place when a competitor's whole livelihood comes from this market space. RIM, the manufacturer of Blackberry cellphones, is likely to fight to the finish because their cellphones are their major product.

The company is likely to have some good competitors who are constantly winning share themselves. Good competitors are a blessing, because these are companies to study, not to go after. You want to figure out—what makes them tick? Who are their marketing experts? And can we entice some of this talent to join our team?

Often there is a competitor coming from a company that drives all of its businesses to be number one or two. Consider Jack Welch's statement when he headed General Electric:

> We believed that only businesses that were number-one or number-two in their markets could win in the increasingly competitive global arena. Those that could not were to be fixed, closed, or sold.

The lesson is: *Don't go after* that *competitor*. He won't tolerate losing a share point. This is a situation where you must accept being a strong follower. This was the historic Ford position vis a vis GM, where Ford found the niche position in Ford pick-up trucks, rather than passenger cars.

Another point to remember: don't be so obsessed with the current competitors that you don't notice *emerging* competitors. For example—auto companies should watch Hyundai:

> Hyundai is showing the fastest growth in car sales among all competitors in both the U.S. and European market. When Toyota and Nissan started to have technology debacles, Hyundai began winning market share. It made quality cars but priced

them lower than competitors in its class, much like Lexus did earlier when it attacked Mercedes. Hyundai offered an unheard of 10 year or 100,000 miles warranty on engines and transmissions. And in 2010, Hyundai offered during the recession to guarantee buyers that the company would take back the car—no questions asked and no credit citation—if the buyer lost his or her job a year after purchase.

Every company should work hard to outperform its competitors by delivering a better offer. The ability to learn and change faster than your competitors may be the only sustainable competitive advantage.

What should ultimately have your attention is not only new technologies emerging, but what is happening to your customers. Customers keep changing. Too many marketers are obsessed with the competition—the enemy—instead of focusing on the customers. If you could choose only between planning to defeat your competitors or trying to do an outstanding job for your customers, choose the latter—as is illustrated next.

Air carrier Jet Blue did an outstanding job by keeping its eye on the customer. Along with other airlines, Jet Blue suffered a sharp decline in traffic when the Great Recession hit. In 2009, the company's revenue was down another 5 percent. However, by 2012, Jet Blue's revenue grew by 18.87 percent. The turnaround came from creating a new travel experience that would sharply bring down the cost of air travel to the customer. Jet Blue installed in their aircraft only nonreclining seats, allowing them to add 40 more seats to the plane. They set an extremely low fare that was 30 percent cheaper than competitors. They added a set of charges: water costs $3. There is an extra charge for using the overhead luggage bin, and a $10 charge for a phone booking. As a result of these and other charges and changes, Jet Blue earns 40 percent more profit per plane. At 85 to 90 percent occupancy per flight, the airline has repackaged the flight experience for super-budget travelers and is making good profits in a low-growth economy.

Conclusion

There can be many culprits that reduce a company's growth: an economic slowdown, a new aggressive competitor in the marketplace, changing buyer tastes, a decline in your brand's freshness, and countless other possibilities. This is a time when your company needs to deeply examine its mission, vision, values, and offerings. The company may have gathered fat in better times; now, it needs to get leaner. You must perform a SWOT analysis to reappraise your main strengths and weaknesses, opportunities and threats. Your company must overcome any weakness in either financial or marketing strength. If it is deficient in both, it might as well retire. Given that the SWOT analysis offers hope, the company must reexamine its marketing mix and profile. It needs to define its target markets more finely, as well as determine from which competitors it can attract new customers. Growth requires not only finding new users and usages for one's offerings, but also determining how to show competitors' customers that your company can present and deliver better results.

Questions

1. How would you describe your growth strategy? Is it based primarily on a keen knowledge of the customers or on wresting share away from your competitors?

2. How well are you prepared defensively? How is your competitive intelligence? Have you implemented an early warning system? Have you ever engaged in a formal scenario planning session—and if so, has it been helpful to you?

3. Does your company know profitability by product, segment, channel, and individual customers? If not, what is the obstacle that's preventing your cost accountant from developing such a system?

4. What would you cut in the event of a double-dip recession?

5. Have you classified your product offerings into yesterday's breadwinners, today's winners, and tomorrow's future winners? Is it desirable for you to reallocate your funds over these different products?

6. To what extent are you able to justify the marketing budget by showing the rate of return on marketing investment? Otherwise, what arguments do you present to justify your budget request?

7. How do you set the market share objective for the coming period and define the separate sources of the planned market share gains?

2 Grow through Developing Committed Customers and Stakeholders

A customer is the most important visitor on our premises. He is not dependent on us—we are dependent on him. He is not an outsider in our business—he is a part of it. We are not doing him a favor by serving him . . . he is doing us a favor by giving us the opportunity to do so.

—L. L. Bean Store in Maine

We said at the end of the last chapter that it is more important to obsess about your customers than to obsess about your competitors. After all, it is customers, not competitors, who determine who wins the war.

We live in a world characterized by an abundance of goods and services. In fact, almost every good is available in oversupply. A car buyer has countless car types and brands to choose from; a mobile handset buyer has a plethora of handset brands to choose from; even a builder of a new factory has so many steel and cement companies to choose from. We are not in a goods shortage economy; rather, we are in a surplus economy. There is only one thing in short supply here: customers. Therefore, the customer is the center of our struggle. So how do we compete for, win, and keep customers?

Because the cost of losing customers and replacing them is much too high, we must learn first and foremost how to keep them. When studying General Motors, John Goodman of TARP—one of the leading specialists on factors in customer satisfaction—found that General Motors had to spend five times as much to attract a new customer as to hold on to an existing one.[1] He estimates that it may cost 20 to 50 times as much for business-to-business (B2B) situations. This is precisely why we need customers to keep coming back to us as a result of being satisfied. However, even satisfying them doesn't guarantee that they won't leave when they get a better offer. We really want to delight them, and turn them into fans and advocates who tell others how good our products and services are. But how do we do that?

There follows another realization: our company is not the only one that affects our customers. Our customers are impacted by our employees, suppliers, distributors, retailers, agents, and word-of-mouth. So how do we make certain that these stakeholder partners are doing their job?

We ask the following questions in examining the "committed customer" pathway to growth:

1. Which customers—and which of their needs—do you want to satisfy?

2. What are the stages that a customer may undergo in becoming more committed and loyal?

3. What can we do to improve our employee impact on customer satisfaction?

4. What can we do to improve our other stakeholders' performance?

Let's look at each in one in more detail.

Which Customers—and Which of Their Needs—Do You Want to Satisfy?

Some companies go after the mass market, assuming that everyone is a potential customer. For instance, Coca-Cola thinks that everyone would find Coke refreshing, and Disney thinks that everyone would enjoy visiting Disneyland. Even so, there are some people who do not like to drink Coke and others who would not want to visit Disneyland. Fortunately, these markets are big enough without these dissenters.

The opposite of a mass market is a micro-market—and there are millions of micro-market segments that all want different things. Exhibit 2.1 shows a set of quite odd and specific micro-markets. Mark Penn, president of renowned polling firm Penn, Schoen and Berland Associates, is brilliant at spotting micro-groups that could be targets for niche marketers. Exhibit 2.1 lists some of Penn's micro-groups, which have been drawn from a much longer list.

Exhibit 2.1 A Sample of 14 Micro Groups Drawn from a List of 76 Micro Groups

Working retireds	Christian Zionists
Stay-at-home workers	Young knitters
Interracial families	Vegan children
Protestant Hispanics	Young tattooed
Sun-haters	Archery moms
Left-handed people	Vietnamese entrepreneurs
Late-breaking gays	Surgery lovers

Source: Mark J. Penn with E. Kinney Zalesne, *Microtrends: The Small Forces Behind Tomorrow's Big Changes*[2] (New York: Twelve, Hachette Book Group, 2007).

Each of these micro-groups is a potential market opportunity. One company might decide to make many different things for left-handed people. A private equity firm might want to focus on investing in Vietnamese entrepreneurs. There are so many groups that might welcome a marketer who cares about them.

However, companies frequently miss these micro-pockets of growth because they're used to thinking only of broad markets. The fact is that there are thousands of pockets of growth in "low-growth economies" just as there are thousands of "pockets of decline" in high-growth markets. An American soap company looking for new business should not go to India just because India has a large population and is having high growth, because the company would find that the soap market is well-served by soap competitors who are already operating in India. The trick is to find some missing needs that soap competitors are not meeting and some areas of India that are relatively underserved by the existing competitors. For example, in the U.S., Burt's Bees is a distinctive and affordable line of personal care products, including soap products, that is widely accessible to the niche of committed natural and organic product consumers. Most companies encounter valuable opportunities by going local and micro, not global and macro. Companies need to decentralize and localize more of their activities. These units of the company are more likely to spot new growth opportunities, and move more quickly to exploit them. The following is an excellent example of a company that keeps track of its customers:

> Clothing retailer Mitchells, based in Greenwich and Westport, Connecticut, is a million-dollar family-owned business that serves an upscale customer base of professional men and women. The company's IBM AS 32 system's database tracks each of its approximately 150,000 customers' personal data and preferences—including size and style, as well as SKUs bought and prices paid. Chairman and CEO Jack Mitchell personally keeps information about his top 1,000 customers at his fingertips. To use his favorite metaphor, the secret to Mitchell's success is "hugging" the customers.
>
> Informational feedback is crucial to helping staff members achieve goals. Every morning, sales associates receive a recap of every sale they made the previous day in their work mailbox. About two weeks after each sale, the database prints out a satisfaction report, which associates use to call their customers and inquire about their shopping experience. Profile reports are prepared daily to gauge how many customers were profiled, and to provide associates with opportunities to update their customers' profiles or ask them for more information. The reports have become a management tool for Mitchells to measure its associates' success.
>
> Mitchells employs nearly 200 people and Jack Mitchell extends his high-touch philosophy to his staff by holding frequent meetings and social events, and extending birthday greetings to their families. Mitchell also personally telephones two key segments: (1) customers who purchased $1,000 per

visit, and (2) new customers. New customers cannot slip by, because they include potential upscale clients who are making a first visit and have to be "hugged" for return purchase.[3]

A key to successful marketing is to figure out what kinds of customers you want to reach, win, and keep. If you fail to define your *target market*, you won't be able to define your *value proposition*. It is not enough to say that your product is "good," "excellent," or "superior"; these terms are devoid of meaning. How, exactly, is your product "good"? Let's say that you sell wall clocks. Do you mean a clock keeps time accurately, or that it can be read from 30 feet, or that it contains an alarm setting, or that it lights in the dark? Obviously, these features will appeal to different customers and it helps to define the type of customers and needs that you want to sell to.

We identify different customer groups by applying *market segmentation*. A market segment is comprised of individuals who have sufficiently similar characteristics, needs, and wants. We can cluster persons into different age groups, income groups, and lifestyle groups. Within a specific age and gender group—say, male teenagers—we can further distinguish "young Metrosexuals," "Technosapiens," "Red-blooded boys," and "Turned inward," among others.[4] If we made blue jeans or sold watches, we would have to adjust our product, price, place, and promotion to each group we choose to serve.

There are always micro-pockets of growth. Just consider the rapid growth of "dollar stores" in a recession economy, or the growing sales of Kia and Hyundai automobiles from South Korea in the U.S. recession economy. When environmentalism becomes as fashionable as economic status, some people decide to buy a smaller, more fuel-efficient car such as a Prius from Toyota instead of a large Cadillac from General Motors. In general, as some businesses decline, others rise during every economic period.

There isn't just one way to break down a market into segments. A smart and creative marketer can imagine a variety of breakdowns, and sometimes spot a new one that opens a host of possibilities. For example, why not segment the dog-food market by the attitude of the dog owner toward the dog—instead of the dog's physical size and age? Some dog owners truly perceive these pets as infants that they need to care for lovingly, feed the best food, and give occasional treats as a reward for learning something new. Other dog owners may see their dog as a companion who keeps them company and simply deserves a good meal. Finally, there is the dog owner who hates the dog, sees it as a burden, and feeds it the cheapest food possible. This segmentation is likely to lead to new ideas for the dog food manufacturer. For example, a dog lover would probably feed the dog the Quantum brand that claims its dog food is free from wheat gluten, soya, beef, and dairy products; rich in oil for healthier skin and coat; and has a low allergy formula for dogs with food-related allergies.

In fact, one major pursuit today is to search for fresh *customer insights*—hopefully, *transformational* insights. One should apply micro-segmentation in the search for unserved *market niches*—a term that typically refers to a small, well-defined group of customers who have a similar need or need set that is usually highly specialized. There are likely only one or two suppliers who would find it profitable to serve that niche. For example, there may be a few hundred homes or restaurants in a large city possessing a tank with tropical fish. These tank owners need to procure the right food to feed the tropical fish—and this food might only be produced by one specialized tropical fish food supplier. This supplier will be well-known to fish tank owners around the world who depend on them. German company Tetra is an example of this, as they have dominant global market share for high-quality tropical fish food.

There are thousands of such niches. Some might be growing, while others are declining or vanishing. But money can be made by niche thinking—for as the expression goes, "In niches there are riches." This doesn't mean that the niche owner or leader should exploit customers' dependency. In fact, niche marketers tend to take good care of their customers because their company is highly dependent on the confidence of this specialized group of consumers.

One safety strategy for a niche owner is to build leading positions in two or three niches, just in case one dries up. Just as an automobile depends on four tires, the owner carries a spare in case one of the tires blows out.

Hermann Simon's excellent book *Hidden Champions* documents the great number of niche-rich companies.[5] Many are highly profitable global businesses that most of us don't know, but they own a major share of a global niche market (see Exhibit 2.2). Simon describes many of these companies and their strategies and his book is an excellent source of ideas.

Exhibit 2.2 Hidden Champions with World Market Shares of 70% or More

Company	Main Product	World Market Share
Dr. Suwelack	Collagen	100%
SkySails	Towing kite wind propulsion systems	100%
Gerriets	Theatre curtains, stage equipment	100%
Ulvac	LCD panel coating	96%
G. W. Barth	Cocoa processing systems	90%

Company	Main Product	World Market Share
GKD-Gebr.Kufferath	Metal fabrics	90%
Kirow Leipzig	Railway cranes	85%
Alki-Technik	Special screw systems	80%
Delo	Adhesives for chip modules on smart cards	80%
Nissha	Small touch panels	80%
ScheBoBiotech	Biotech in in-vitro diagnostics	80%
Kern-Liebers	Spring for safety belts	80%
Weckerie	Lipstick machines	80%
TEXPA	Home textile processing machines	75%
Achenbach Buschhutten	Aluminum rolling mills, rolling mill filtration systems	70%
Karl Mayer	Warp knitting machines	70%
Omicron	Tunnel-grid/tunnel-probe microscopes	70%
Tente Rollen	Casters for hospital beds	70%
Wirtgen	Road-recycling machines	70%

Source: Hermann Simon, *Hidden Champions of the 21st Century*, Springer, Bonn-Germany, 2009, p. 73.

Many entrepreneurs think that the best opportunities lie in pursuing new industries, especially in digital space. But you never want to make the mistake of discounting old industries. Steel is an old industry, and while many large integrated steel companies are suffering, Nucor and other mini-mills have given new life to the steel industry.

Consider the example of the 900-year-old coffee industry, which started in Ethiopia, moved to Turkey, and then made its way to Europe. Most of us buy our coffee in cans in the supermarket or order coffee in a restaurant. But a multibillion-dollar coffee business was built in the past 24 years—Starbucks—due to Howard Schultz, who in 1988 imagined a new vision for serving a worldwide "rich rewarding coffee experience," which is Starbucks' marketing mantra.

Similarly, bookstores have been around ever since Gutenberg invented a new way of printing back in the mid-1400s. All the bookstores that emerged during the 600 years following were quite small, crowded with shelves and books, and little else. A few may have served coffee—but no service innovation occurred until Leonard Riggio purchased the Barnes and Noble bookstore in New York City in 1971 and introduced discount book prices. Riggio went further and made a bookstore a destination not only for book buyers but for people seeking a comfortable place to sit, meet with friends, have coffee and pastry, and listen to talks on books.

Toy companies have been making baby dolls for little girls for hundreds of years; they even became a collectible item. But it took the Mattel Company to introduce the Barbie doll, which has become the most profitable toy ever. Barbie is not the traditional baby doll that had been sold before, but an attractive young lady sold in all countries and in all types of clothing. As such, it became a collectible toy to young girls around the world.

Families have been able to enjoy pizza for hundreds of years—either by making it at home or going out to a pizza restaurant. But it was Dominos Pizza chain, started in the 1960s, that thought of delivering a hot freshly made pizza to the customer's home within one half hour of the phone order—if late, there would be no charge. Tom Monaghan and his company deserve the credit for fresh thinking in this otherwise mature industry.

Postal service was well established in most countries for hundreds of years. Citizens would use the postal system to send mail—expecting it to be delivered within a few days—or a week at the most. No one even imagined that the post office could deliver mail overnight—that is, until Fred Smith established

Federal Express in April 1973. He had conceived of overnight delivery of mail while a student at Yale, but his professor thought that it was an impractical idea. Smith conceived that all mail would be delivered to a central hub—Memphis, Tennessee—each evening and sorted and sent to their proper destinations for arrival the next morning before 10:30 A.M. FedEx changed the speed at which we can mail letters and packages forever.

This is all reminiscent of Theodore Levitt's famous 1960 *Harvard Business Review* article about mature industries.[6] Levitt had simply heard too many managers claiming that they couldn't grow more because their industries were too "mature." His take: Calling your industry mature is self-defeating and shows a lack of marketing imagination.

Our message: Every mature industry is worth reexamining for potential new ideas.

What Are the Stages That a Customer Might Pass Through in Becoming More Loyal?

All first-time customers buy with a certain set of expectations about the product/service they're purchasing—and the company supplying it. If these expectations are met or exceeded, customers are likely to buy again from the same supplier. The company might hope that the customer moves through the following stages:

Satisfied customer → Committed customer → Customer advocate → Customer co-creator → Customer owner

Companies would be wise to avoid boasting about their "satisfied customers." Cadillac lost a great deal of market share despite high "customer satisfaction" scores when Mercedes and BMW came along. This teaches an important lesson: a company must do more than just *satisfy* a customer.

Satisfied customers are likely to turn into committed customers when they receive substantially *more* satisfaction than expected. The aim is—and should always be—to *delight* the customer. In order to achieve this, a product must perform substantially better than competitive products. The staff must show a special interest in the customer and respond quickly and thoughtfully to customer requests. The company must be generous in handling returns or in giving advice.

Several companies are known to have developed enthusiastic and delighted customers. One only has to walk into an Apple store to see the crowds of enthusiastic customers trying out the new products. Or ask any Harley-Davidson motorcycle owner how he feels about the motorcycle he rides. Or ask military personnel who do banking and insurance with USAA about their level of delight with the company. Or ask Enterprise-Rent-a-Car customers how they feel about the service this brand provides to them.

Your committed customers are the best ones to consider in planning your future offerings, since you know those customers—not your non-customers. You have to ask: What else can I do for my customers? What other needs do they have that I can satisfy? Here is an excellent example of a company that asked—and adequately answered—these questions:

Euclid is a four-generation family commercial cleaning business in the Cleveland area, with a high touch personal relationship to customers. To keep its loyal staff in the declining Cleveland industrial market, Euclid launched lateral services that range from original basic commercial cleaning to janitorial work, industrial cleaning, carpet cleaning, wall washing, floor maintenance, acoustic ceiling cleaning, construction cleanup, duct cleaning, walk-off mat rental service and sales—really, meeting just about any request a client makes. Cleveland area clients have asked Euclid to open service centers in new cities where they are expanding. General Electric has taken Euclid Industrial Maintenance crews to Anaheim, Atlanta, St. Louis, New Orleans, Tampa, and Mobile. Because of their flexibility and response to client needs, Euclid is looking into a future that includes further specialization into various areas—such as construction cleanup, kitchen cleaning, hood and duct cleaning and maintenance, and a continued reliance on what started it all—window cleaning and janitorial work.[7]

A customer who is committed to a company is most likely to agree to be a *customer advocate*—even if not asked outright. The question you must ask, however, is: Would you feel comfortable recommending our company to friends and acquaintances? This question was proposed by business author Frederick Reichheld in his December 2003 *Harvard Business Review* article entitled "One Number You Need to Grow."[8] Reichheld recommended that companies score their customers' answers to the question on a scale from 1 to 10. They would give a 10 if the customer has been recommending your company regularly; a 9 if the customer has done so occasionally; an 8 if the customer says he or she would feel comfortable to do this; and continue all the way down to a 1 for the customer who says that he or she actually *dislikes* your company and would even tell friends to avoid it. A score called the *Net Promotion Score* is derived by taking the percentage of scores of 8, 9, or 10 and then subtracting the percentage of scores from 1 to 6. Presumably, the higher the net promotion score, the higher the positive word of mouth—and therefore, that company's profitability—is likely to be.

A customer advocate might even turn into a customer co-creator. This would be a customer who wants to get involved in helping improve the company's products, services, advertisements, and so on. Consider those Harley-Davidson fans that Harley invites to hang around with the organization's engineers to suggest improvements in the motorcycle. Another example is the youngsters in Denmark who ask Lego if they can help the brand's designers build new Lego structures—or Dorito's snack enthusiasts who submitted thousands of proposed Dorito advertising campaigns for the company to consider.

In a book called *The Ownership Quotient*, authors and business experts James Heskett, Earl Sasser, and Joe Wheeler offer a definition of the highest level of customer that they call a "customer owner": "A *customer owner* is one who tries a product or service, is so satisfied that she returns to buy more, states a willingness to tell others of her experiences, actually convinces others to buy, provides constructive criticism of existing offerings, and even suggests or helps test new products or ideas." The real sign of a company that is achieving customer bonding is the percentage of their customers that the company can call "customer owners."[9]

Now, the challenge is to determine which actions companies can take to increase the number of loyal and enthusiastic customers. Several books have been written about this—including those with such titles as *Creating Customer Evangelists, The Power of Cult Branding,* and *Creating Raving Fans*.[10] These books discuss methods including differentiation, customization, personalization, experiences creation, exceptional service, and creating a fan-based community that helped churches, sports teams, and entertainers create loyal fans. Exhibit 2.3 lists several actions that promise to produce more loyal customers.

*Exhibit 2.3 Actions That Produce More
Loyal Customers*

1. Extraordinary service

2. Extraordinary guarantees

3. Customer training and consulting

4. Supplying software/hardware

5. Offering entertainment/gifts

6. Managing the customer's complexity

7. Frequency award programs

8. Club membership programs

All of these represent promising ways for your company to differentiate itself and customize relationships with your customers. In his book *Strategic Customer Service*, author John Goodman mentioned two examples of the kind of high touch that matters most to customers.[11] One was Allstate Insurance, who knew that many of their policyholders worry about their teenage drivers. So they mailed a brochure to parents of teenagers on "How to Talk to Your Kid About Driving"—a move that customers appreciated greatly. In another example, an American Auto Association (AAA) driver pulled up to a female driver waiting in a hot car that needed to be towed. Before doing anything else, he first handed her a cold bottle of water and apologized for the delay—even though he was early. The little things in life can make a big difference.

What Can Be Done to Improve Our Employees' Impact on Customer Satisfaction?

Customers are influenced by *everything* they see and hear when dealing with a company. They sense the atmosphere within the building or store, and they take notice of employees' attitudes and helpfulness. This is precisely why companies need to carefully select the people they hire, and put them through a well-thought-out customer training program. Disney is a model company in this regard; they select staff members carefully and have them undergo a week-long (and sometimes longer) training program before they meet and greet a single visitor entering Disneyland. The Four Seasons hotel is another brand that is renowned for spending considerable time in selecting and training its employees in "Putting Guests First."

What kinds of attitudes toward customers should companies try to put into their employees' thinking and behavior? Exhibit 2.4 presents a collection of "customer importance statements" that companies should share with their employees.

Exhibit 2.4 Customer Importance Statements

- The purpose of a company is "to create a customer. . . . The only profit center is the customer" (Peter Drucker).
- "A customer who complains is my best friend" (Stew Leonard).
- "Rule 1: The customer is always right. Rule 2: If the customer is ever wrong, read Rule 1" (Stew Leonard).

- "The customer is the only one who can fire us all" (Sam Walton).
- "The best way to hold your customers is to constantly figure out how to give them more for less" (Jack Welch).
- "You've got a new boss . . . the customer. If you're not thinking customer, you're not thinking" (Anonymous).
- "Never underestimate the power of the irate customer" (Joel E. Ross and Michael J. Kami).
- "If we're not customer-driven, our cars won't be, either" (Ford Motor).
- "Make a customer, not a sale" (Katherine Barchetti).
- "Every client you keep, is one less that you need to find" (Niger Sanders).
- "The purpose of a business is to create a customer who creates customers" (Sriv Singh).
- "Good customer service costs less than bad customer service" (Sally Gronow).
- Customer service is not a department, it's everyone's job (Anonymous).
- "Strive to find out what the customer likes and do more of it; strive to find out what the customer dislikes and do less of it" (Anonymous).
- "The best companies don't create customers; they create fans" (Ken Blanchard).
- "Instead of seeing a customer in every individual, we should see an individual in every customer" (Jan Carlson).

(continued)

- "Always try to satisfy the toughest customers; then it will be easy to satisfy the rest" (Anonymous).

- "If you can't smile, don't open a store" (Chinese proverb).

Companies that succeed with their employees see the development of superior customer service as an "internal marketing" task. They treat employees in the same way that they want employees to treat customers; they care and ask about employees' needs, wants, values, and satisfaction. They want to establish pay, hours, expectations, and social settings in a way that is congruent with employee needs and desires. They want employees to *enjoy* working for their company, to think highly of its products and service quality, to see the company as well managed, and to be proud to work there. Each year, a variety of magazines publish lists of "the best companies to work for"—information that's gathered from surveys of the actual employees working in various companies. And it doesn't come as much of a surprise that those seeking jobs would generally prefer to apply to the companies that have a high employee satisfaction ranking.

Clearly, most organizations would hope to have a large percentage of highly motivated employees—those who would fit the description of "employee owners." Namely, they desire a situation wherein "*Employee owners* exhibit their sense of ownership through loyalty, referrals of other high-potential employees, and suggestions for improving the quality of processes and work life as well as the organization's overall effectiveness in serving customers."[12]

In spite of these efforts, there will still be differences in terms of employees' customer relations skills. Staff members are likely to be distributed into the five employee commitment categories shown in Exhibit 2.5.[13]

Exhibit 2.5 Five Employee Commitment Categories

Employee Ambassadors (Advocates)– the most active level, this represents employees who are strongly committed to the companys's brand promise, the organization itself, and its customers. Also, importantly, they behave and communicate in a consistently positive manner towards the company, both inside and outside.

Positive Loyalists– employees who exhibit positive feelings about their job and emotional kinship with the company. They are favorable about the company overall, have every intention of remaining there, and actively and positively perform on its behalf. Though they don't frequently communicate about the company, the messages they do communicate are largely positive.

Positive Contributors– employees who are generally satisfied with their jobs but rather ambivalent to mildly positive about the company overall, their relationship with it, and its products. They may communicate some generally positive messages about the company to others, but they do so rarely and inconsistently.

Disinterested Seat Fillers– employees who lack interest in, favorability towards, or kinship with the company and its products. They either do not communicate positive messages about the company internally or externally, or do not communicate at all. For minimally involved members of staff, employment with the company is 'just a job', and very little more.

Employee Saboteurs– employees who, though still drawing a paycheck from the company, are active and frequently vocal detractors about the organization itself, its culture and policies, and its products and services. These individuals are negative advoates, communicating their unflattering opinions and unfavorable perspectives to both peers inside the company and to customers, and others, outside the company.

The various levels depicted above make it clear that companies need to monitor their various employees' behavior. Those in the last three categories do little to build loyal customers, and in fact can easily cause a company to lose loyal customers. This is one of the reasons why it is critical to conduct periodic employee performance reviews. The problem is only exacerbated when obstacles prevent companies from terminating those employees who are performing poorly.

In an effort to motivate the people who work for them, some companies have replaced the term "employees" with other terms, such as "associates" or "partners"—anything to give the employees a sense of ownership in the company or in its results. *Fortune* magazine conducts an extensive poll each year to rate the 100 Best Companies to Work For. The top 10 results for 2012 were (in order) Google, Boston Consulting Group, SAS Institute, Wegman's Food Markets, Edward Jones, NetApp, Camden Property Trust, Recreational Equiment (REI), CHG Healthcare Services, and Quicken Loans.[14]

What Can We Do to Improve Our Other Stakeholders' Performance?

Your customers are constantly impacted by other stakeholders—including distributors, retailers, agents, brokers, advertising agencies, and other suppliers. We must work with these various outlets to manage a co-dependent supply chain leading to the final customer.

Consider a chain such as Denny's Restaurants, which operates 1,500 U.S. outlets, has 47,000 employees, is open 24 hours a day, and serves 150 entrees to one million customers each day. Denny's challenge is determining how to achieve high service quality throughout the system—from greeting customers, cooking, cleaning tables, washing dishes, to accepting payment, as well as provisions and equipment suppliers. In order to do this, they depend very much on *all* their suppliers in the chain.

All this goes back to the fact that every company is a *people* business. The company's stakeholders are people, and people carry all sorts of values, wishes, dreams, and burdens. Therefore, every single organization must figure out what each stakeholder group values and to do its best to meet their expectations.

Without trying to provide answers, we do need to make one thing clear: a company's success depends on much more than the company itself. It depends on the company's collection of stakeholders and their quality and motivation. If Levi's is working with a better and more motivated set of stakeholders than its competitor, Wrangler, then Levi's is likely to outperform Wrangler in the marketplace.

Conclusion

The more accurately you can define your target customers and develop a winning offer, the more likely it is that your customers will prefer doing business with you. Your cost of serving customers who are already loyal to you is much less than the cost of searching for new customers to replace those that you lose. The goal is to move your customers into higher stages in the continuum—from satisfied customer to committed customer to customer advocate to customer co-creator to customer owner. To succeed, you also need to move your employees into high stages in the continuum—from disinterested seat fillers, to passive contributors, and finally to employee ambassadors. The same can be said for moving up your suppliers and distributors into higher stages of commitment.

Questions

1. Describe one of your customer target groups. How well have you defined this group? Should you broaden or narrow this definition?

2. Have you estimated the cost of a lost customer, and the cost of replacing such a customer? Discuss the implications.

3. Suppose you could undertake an effort to improve customer loyalty (see Exhibit 2.3). Describe the effort. What would it cost? What would be the expected return?

4. What percentage of your customers would you call *committed* to you? Are they satisfied? How many are delighted? What could you do to increase this percentage?

5. Would you say that a sufficient number of your employees are highly committed and acting as employee owners? If not, why not? What policies can you establish to improve employee loyalty?

6. How can you get channel members on the supply and distribution side to feel more like *partners*?

3 Grow by Developing a Powerful Brand

A brand for a company is like a reputation for a person. You can earn reputation by trying to do hard things well.

—Jeff Bezos, Amazon

Every company is a brand, even if it doesn't do any outright branding activity. The sheer fact that the company exists and engages in buying and selling creates an image in the minds of everyone who hears about or does business with the company. These people are likely able to mention one or more things about the company. If there is a lot of image convergence, we could say that the company carries a well-defined brand image. The only question is whether the company is satisfied with its brand image—or would like to manage it better. A company undertakes conscious branding when it wants to establish a certain reputation—one that has power and consistency in the marketplace.

This doesn't mean that the company is trying to project the same image to every group. McDonald's, for example, aims a slightly different message to mothers, teenagers, and senior citizens as to why they might come eat at their restaurants.

If aircraft maker Boeing is trying to win a contract from United Airlines, it will emphasize different qualities when it talks to the company's engineers, purchasing people, chief financial officer, and CEO—since each United participant will consider different matters during the purchase process. The company needs its brand messages to be compatible and consistent with the overall understanding of Boeing.

We actually need to distinguish three separate brand concepts here: brand *integrity*, brand *identity*, and brand *image*. The planning must start with brand integrity, since this is where the company honestly assesses what it is capable of delivering and fulfilling for its customers and its prospects. Brand integrity is the company's promise of value, and it is the key to creating customer trust. From this basis, the company can move to designing its brand identity—namely, spelling out how the company wants others to see it. Brand identity involves positioning as a certain type of company. The next step is to decide on the company's brand image; namely, how the company appears to differ from its competitors. Without signifying differentiation, the company's image would be the same as another undifferentiated competitor or invisible against a differentiated competitor. Further steps will take place later to work out the specific brand elements and visuals.

Let's apply this brand planning sequence to Timberland (see Exhibit 3.1), a company that makes outdoor footwear and apparel. Timberland's brand integrity rests on its early innovative technology of molded footwear and the fact that it was the first branded bootware in the U.S. Timberland gets its brand identity by positioning itself in the class of those outdoor brands that can create and carry inspired footwear and apparel. But it then builds its brand image by differentiators such as being an engaged corporate citizen, being a steward of the environment, and fighting for global human rights. As it turns out, Timberland is highly regarded by its stakeholders and has won a huge following.

Exhibit 3.1   The Three I Model Illustrated for Timberland

While companies put in a lot of work in designing their brand image, they don't always get precisely what they want—since many forces outside of their control can also affect their image. Consider the brand image of Walmart—a store that was originally all about having the lowest prices. When Walmart was later criticized about failing to care about their environmental impact, it undertook positive actions and added a layer of environmental responsibility to its image. As such, Walmart is changing its truck fleet to lower carbon emission vehicles and also encouraging its suppliers to buy and use more fuel-efficient trucks if they still want Walmart's business. Then, when the company received criticism about its low wages and poor employee treatment, it took steps to improve its employment practices. Clearly, a company has to consider refreshing its practices and image as new issues arise. More recently, Walmart was alleged with using bribery to get new locations in Mexico—another thing that has hurt the brand. The lesson is clear: as carefully as a company might try to *design* its image, one's reputation is always subject to forces beyond its control. In this case, a company's best course of action is to respond quickly.

There are many companies that make products that draw criticism—all the way from tobacco and alcoholic beverage companies to brands like McDonald's and Coca-Cola who are charged with heavily contributing to American's rising level of obesity. These are the very companies that do their best to support good causes and show responsible citizenship—efforts that are designed to build a bank of goodwill. These companies don't know when the next Ralph Nader will draw huge attention to their social harm and put them on the defensive. So they hope that they've won enough friends through their philanthropy to keep their brand under damage control.

Given the high potential contributions that branding can make to growth, we ask you to consider the following questions:

1. In what ways does developing a strong brand increase a company's growth potential?

2. Can *everything* be branded?

3. What elements make up a company's brand?

4. What are the characteristics of a strong brand?

5. What are the main tools for building a brand?

6. How far can a brand be stretched before losing its meaning?

7. How can a company track whether its brand equity is rising or falling?

8. What is the digital impact on brand building and control?

Let's look at each one.

In What Ways Does Developing a Strong Brand Increase the Company's Growth Potential?

A strong brand helps a company grow in three specific ways. First, these companies can charge a higher price—which hopefully leads to higher profits, thereby resulting in more cash to expand the business further. For instance, since Caterpillar has a very strong name in the construction equipment category, it can charge more—because buyers know of Caterpillar's great product and service quality. In earning more, it can grow faster.

Secondly, a company with a strong name has an easier time getting into distribution channels. You can find Coca-Cola in supermarkets, vending machines, gas stations, restaurants, and many other venues. Imagine, however, whether a new drink with an unknown name would have much of a chance to be carried in most venues. A brand name's strength determines how quickly and successfully a company can expand its business.

Third, once the brand gains trust and respect, companies can put that same brand name on—and then launch—more new items. This is why Campbell Soup Company doesn't need to invent a new brand name for each new soup that it launches. The fact that the distinct, recognizable Campbell's name is on the soup gives both the buyer and the distribution channels confidence in the product. Not needing to develop a new brand name saves the company a considerable amount of money. And because it is easier to launch new products under the same name, the company can achieve much faster market penetration.

It is hard to underestimate the importance of a strong brand in relation to the company's other assets. A senior manager at Coca-Cola once said that he would prefer to sell all the factories, equipment, and other company assets—as long as he could keep the company's name. We understand this: Brand consultancy Interbrand estimated that Coca-Cola is worth $71 billion in brand value in its 2011 Ranking of the Top 100 brands. It was followed by IBM ($70 billion), Microsoft ($59 billion), Google ($55 billion), and GE ($43 billion).[1]

What can a brand do to stay profitable during a recession? Here are some realistic possibilities:

- Add a *lower-price item with fewer features* to your product line. You might even launch it under a different brand name. Most companies should produce a line of products at different price points.

- Add some *additional value to the offer*, such as free shipping or installation.

- Maintain the current price but *advertise heavily as to why customers should pay more* for this brand. Procter & Gamble (P&G) uses this strategy with Tide, instead of cutting the price.

- Change the *brand's image through a new campaign*. Dove introduced its "Real Beauty" campaign in China in 2011 based on the notion that most women have real beauty—and Dove can help them realize it.

- *Innovate something new*. Apple introduced its iPhone just before the Great Recession and caused Nokia's market share to decline from 50 percent to 10 percent in five years.

- Shift to win the low price position but *maintain the brand value and promise*. Insurance provider Geico sells auto insurance mainly online and, as a well-known brand, owns the low-cost position.

Can Everything Be Branded?

The answer is yes: *everything* can be branded. Even more importantly—everything can potentially benefit from a *conscious* branding effort. For examples of the countless items, services, and even people that have been branded, see Exhibit 3.2.

Exhibit 3.2 Everything Can Be Branded

- *Consumer Products:* Absolut Vodka, Barbie Doll, BMW, Kleenex
- *Industrial Products:* Pentium chip, HP Laserjet, DuPont Nylon
- *Services:* Avis, Federal Express, Disney, Club Med, Weight Watchers
- *Retailers:* Marks & Spencer, Walmart, Boots, Walgreen's, Home Depot
- *Corporations:* IBM, GE, Intel, Apple, Nestlé, Samsung
- *People:* Madonna, Calvin Klein, Barbra Streisand
- *Places:* Paris "City of Light," Chicago "Second City," Silicon Valley "Tech Capital"
- *Commodities:* California oranges, Idaho potatoes, Dasani water, Perdue chicken, Chiquita bananas, Acme bricks

---

There is a difference between a retailer claiming that a store sells computers and that it sells Apple computers—since Apple computers sell for 10 to 20 percent more than their competitors. There is a difference between a supermarket selling fresh chicken and selling *Perdue* chicken, since the brand name sells for 15 percent more. Even commodities are named—think of Idaho potatoes, Evian water, Chiquita bananas, and Acme bricks.

What Elements Make Up the Company's Brand?

Some people think of a brand as merely a name put on an object—and that *was* the original meaning when we said that a steer was to be branded with the owner's name. But if a brand is to mean anything today, it must be much more than a name. At the very least, a brand should carry the following elements: name, logo, and slogan.

Name   Choosing a brand name is very important. I don't know if actor Alan Alda would have been as popular a movie star if he kept his original name of Alphonso D'Abruzzo. I am more interested in having kiwi fruit than Chinese gooseberry, its former name; and I'm much happier vacationing in Paradise Island than Hog Island.

A product's name should not be an afterthought, because you have to live with it—or go through great expense to change it. And you can draw the name from many sources:

- *Names of Founders*—William E. Boeing, John Deere, Paul Julius Reuter, Werner von Siemens, and John Pierpont Morgan.
- *Descriptive Names*—British Airways, Airbus, Caterpillar, Deutsche Telekom, International Business Machines, and General Electric.

- *Acronyms*—IBM, BASF, BBDO, DHL, HP, HSBC, SAP, and UPS.
- *Fabricated Names*—Accenture, Exxon Mobil, Xerox.
- *Metaphors*—Apple, Virgin.

You should test your product's potential name against a list of certain desirable characteristics. We say that a successfully chosen name would have six characteristics (see Exhibit 3.3): the first three (memorable, meaningful, and likable) can be characterized as *brand building* in terms of how brand equity can be built through the judicious choice of a brand element. The latter three (transferable, adaptable, and protectable) are more *defensive* and are concerned with how the brand equity contained in a brand element can be leveraged and preserved in the face of different opportunities and constraints.

---

*Exhibit 3.3 Choice Criteria for
Naming the Brand*

- Memorable
- Meaningful
- Likable
- Transferable
- Adaptable
- Protectable

You can test your proposed brand name against each of these criteria. One thing to be careful about is the name's transferability and translation—especially if you plan to use it overseas in different languages. Consider the following problems that companies encountered with their brand name:

- Chevrolet's Nova car didn't sell well in Spanish speaking countries, because "no va" means "it doesn't go" in Spanish.

- Japan's Mitsubishi Motors had to rename its Pajero model in Spanish-speaking countries because the term related to masturbation.

- Toyota Motors' MR2 model dropped the number in France because the combination sounded like a French swear word.

- When Braniff Airlines translated a slogan touting its upholstery, "Fly in leather," it came out in Spanish as "Fly naked."

- When Pepsi started marketing its products in China a few years back, the Chinese translation of their slogan, "Pepsi Brings You Back to Life," came out as "Pepsi Brings Your Ancestors Back from the Grave."

- When Coca-Cola was first shipped to China, it named the product something that when pronounced sounded like "Coca-Cola." The only problem was that the characters used meant "Bite the wax tadpole." Coca-Cola later switched to a set of characters that mean "Happiness in the mouth."

- Hair product company Clairol introduced a curling iron called the "Mist Stick," into Germany—only to find out that *mist* means "manure."

Logo After the company chooses a brand name, it needs to hire a designer to give the name a strong visual identity. It then chooses a logo—a symbol or emblem that normally embodies the company name (see Exhibit 3.4). Occasionally, the name is not even mentioned—as in the famous Apple logo showing a partly eaten apple.

Exhibit 3.4 A Variety of Company Logos

Slogan   I would advise that a company add a slogan to further communicate something about the company. The slogan presents a short statement to help someone remember the company's products. The following are some well-known slogans:

- Nike: "Just do it."
- BMW: "Ultimate Driving Machine."
- Quaker Oats: "Warms your heart and soul."
- Coca-Cola: "The Real Thing."
- Emerson: "Consider It Solved."
- GE: "Imagination at Work" or "We Bring Good Things to Life."

- Hewlett Packard: "Invent."
- Xerox: "The Document Company."
- Budweiser: "King of Beers."

A company must choose its slogan carefully so that it doesn't backfire by creating disbelief. Ford has used for many years the slogan "Quality is our #1 job," and yet the list of the top 10 automobiles ranked highest in quality didn't include Ford. Holiday Inn sought to assure guests that the hotel is run well and used the slogan "No Surprises." But guests weren't amused when they couldn't find a towel or reach an operator. Holiday Inn dropped this slogan shortly after starting it. Lloyds Bank had to drop its new slogan, "The Bank That Likes to Say Yes," after refusing loans to a number of applicants. Dutch company Philips Electronics, one of the largest electronics companies in the world, went through a number of slogan changes ("From Sand to Chips," to "Philips Invents for You," to "Let's Make Things Better" as each previous one failed).

A longer statement is usually called a tagline. This is a phrase that says something about the content, such as:

- Aetna: "The Company You Need for the Life You Want"
- MasterCard: "There are some things money cannot buy. For everything else, there's MasterCard."

Again, be sure to check carefully how your slogan will translate in a foreign language—and don't make the mistakes these two companies did:

- When Coors translated its slogan "Turn it loose" into Spanish, it was read as "Suffer from diarrhea."
- Chicken magnate Frank Perdue's line, "It takes a tough man to make a tender chicken," sounds much more interesting in Spanish: "It takes a sexually stimulated man to make a chicken affectionate."

Other Elements of a Brand   You can further enrich a brand by adding a few more elements—one of which is *color*. For example, Caterpillar uses the color yellow on all of its earth-moving equipment; Coca Cola has always used the color red on its packaging. It even tried to trademark the color. A company may feature a certain *sound, music*, or *jingle* to accompany its name when it appears, in the way that AOL opens its software with a male voice saying "Welcome. You've got mail!" or George Gershwin's "Rhapsody in Blue" has been used as a brand theme by United Airlines since 1976. Some companies feature a certain *character*. Kentucky Fried Chicken outlets show a picture of Colonel Saunders while ads for Traveler's Insurance feature an umbrella as a symbol. There is more interest now in the brand affecting all the senses including seeing, hearing, tasting, smelling, and touching.[2] High-end retailers such as Tiffany and Hermès do their best to stimulate all the senses in building their brand experience, which may include aesthetic lighting features and enchanting aromas.

Building an impressive brand takes a Creative Marketer who also works with a Design group—especially with someone who specializes in Visual Identity. Design and Marketing need to work as partners—not only on the elements and branding impact, but on the whole physical product or process that a company is proffering to the market. We would go so far as to say that Apple's success with its products and branding owes as much to brilliant design as to brilliant marketing.

What Are the Characteristics of a Strong Brand?

Even if we know what elements a brand needs, we can't always tell what will make something into a respected and widely known "super brand." What keeps brands such as Coca-Cola, Virgin, BMW, Mercedes, and other great ones going?

Brazil would like to know the answer, since they have few well-known brands worldwide. Yet the country is the world's largest grower of coffee beans, which they sell to a Swiss company that doesn't grow coffee. The Swiss company gets 10 times as much for this coffee as it paid the Brazilians—and this company is called Nestlé. Why can't the Brazilians develop a brand for their coffee, charge less, and make all the profit? The answer is simple: they don't have the name Nescafé.

Marketing research consultants Millward Brown and WPP have developed the BRANDZ model of brand strength, at the heart of which is the BrandDynamics pyramid (see Exhibit 3.5).

Exhibit 3.5 BrandDynamics Model of Brand Building

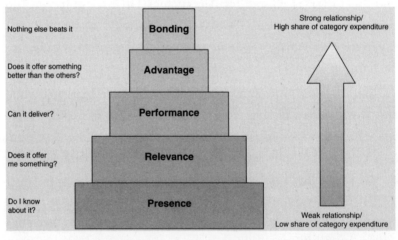

According to this model, brand building involves five steps—each step of which is contingent upon successfully accomplishing the previous step with consumers. The company uses different tools to accomplish each step. Thus, while ads are necessary to get people to know about the brand—and can help in some other steps—they probably only play a small role in the last two steps. Making a trial offer is helpful in the third and fourth steps, and strong commitment to serve the customer continuously and well would help bring about the fifth step.

The company's goal should be to create bonded (that is, committed) consumers who will spend more of their category expenditures on this brand and talk more favorably about it. However, you'll find most consumers at the lower levels. The challenge for marketers is to develop activities and programs that help consumers move up the pyramid.

Advertising agency Young and Rubicam (Y&R) has developed another model consisting of the four variables shown in Exhibit 3.6.

Exhibit 3.6 Brand Asset Valuator Model

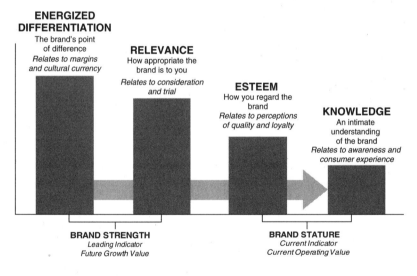

Source: Brand Asset Valuator (BAV), Property of Young & Rubicam Group, WPP PLC.

Y&R calls its model the Brand Asset Valuator (BAV for short). It has been researched with almost 500,000 consumers in

44 countries and covers thousands of brands across hundreds of different categories. The four variables are the pillars of brand equity, the most important of which is *energized differentiation* (or momentum). This quality indicates that the brand is highly differentiated and has momentum. Apple Computer currently has this momentum—something that anyone who enters any one of its stores—that are always packed with consumers intrigued with the Apple Mac computers, iPods, iPads, and iPhones—can clearly see. Relevance is the second major contributor. Facebook has high relevance today. The combination of relevance and energized differentiation constitutes *brand strength* . Esteem (Merck, for example) and Knowledge (IBM, for example) together create *Brand Stature*, which is more of a report card on past performance. By measuring these variables on thousands of brands, Y&R claims that it can tell which brands will experience strong growth—and which will lag.

What Are the Main Tools for Building a Brand?

Building the brand is not just the marketing department's job; it is the whole company's responsibility. A poor employee, supplier, partner, or distributor will hurt the brand's esteem. But it is the marketing group that is responsible for defining the brand's identity. We often say that whereas the product is created in the factory, the brand's meaning is created in the marketing department. Charles Revson of cosmetics brand Revlon said it well: "In the factory, we make the product; in the store, we sell hope."[3]

Many people who are new to marketing think that building a brand is primarily a matter of getting enough money to pay for

30-second television commercials. While we admit to the
usefulness of TV advertising for a mass marketed product, it
would be myopic to think that we can only build brands with TV
advertising—or for that matter, print, radio and billboard
advertising. Exhibit 3.7 lists a whole range of tools that can create
awareness, interest, knowledge, consideration, and even
preference for a newly launched brand.

Exhibit 3.7 Tools for Building a Brand

- Traditional and digital advertising
- Social media presence
- Sponsorships of events and causes
- Creating clubs/user communities
- Visits to the company
- Visits to trade shows
- Traveling exhibits
- Webcasts of presentations, roundtables, entertainment
- Opening stores or showrooms
- Contributing public facilities or backing social causes
- Offering high value for the money

Clearly, marketers can draw on many tools to win attention
and create preference in the target market. The choice they make
depends on the relative coverage and productivities of the various
tools in relation to their costs.

How Far Can a Brand Be Stretched Before It Risks Losing Its Meaning?

Companies that build strong brands are often tempted to use them to launch new products. But how far can the company stretch a brand name without having it lose its meaning? Nike's brand name is found on its athletic footwear and athletic apparel—but not on men's suits. It is okay to use the brand name where the products have some relation to each other. On the other hand, no one would buy a General Motors shampoo—nor would a shampoo company name its shampoo General Motors.

We need to distinguish between (1) producing brand variants in the same category (line extension); (2) stretching into another category (brand extension); and (3) stretching into another industry (brand stretch).

Line extension is the most frequently found application of repeating the use of the brand name. Campbell's is the name given to each new soup that Campbell introduces; Kellogg's is the name given to each new cereal that Kellogg introduces; and Mercedes is the name given to each new car that Mercedes introduces.

Brand *extension* is used to describe occasions when you put your brand name on items that you are introducing in *another* category. For example, Harley-Davidson puts its name not only on its famed motorcycles but on other items that its club members (called Hogs: Harley Owner Groups) might normally buy to show their Harley identity. Harley owners can have a Harley pen, watch, wallet, leather jacket, T-shirt, and even visit a Harley-Davidson Cafe in Las Vegas, Nevada. But in spite of covering a number of items in other categories, Harley still won't put its name on very distant products—such as a Harley baby crib or Harley diamond ring.

Brand *stretch* takes place where a company will enter *any industry* using its brand name. The best example of this is Virgin. Founder Richard Branson first started this name in the music business, then used it to enter a number of other industries—including soft drinks, cell phones, railroads, an airline, wedding gowns, and others. However, Branson doesn't just blindly jump into categories; he only enters industries when he can offer superior quality, something innovative, or a sense of fun and cheekiness. His Virgin Atlantic airline was the first to serve ice cream and to offer massages, and it wouldn't surprise me if he introduced a casino or exercise space on his airline. To launch his Virgin bridal-wear brand, Branson dressed in drag as a bride.

The message is clear: when a company has built a strong brand, it must proceed carefully in extending or stretching it. Yet the company doesn't have control over what others might do with the brand name. In the Internet Age, more people will be talking to more of their acquaintances about both their good and bad experiences with brands. Companies need to monitor what others are saying; they must try to take advantage of the good word of mouth and take actions to correct the bad. And all companies should consider using Google Alert to follow the talk online—not only to find out what people are saying about their own brand, but also to uncover conversations about competitors.

How Can a Company Track Whether Its Brand Equity Is Rising or Falling?

It makes sense for the CEO to ask brand managers whether their brand's strength and stature is rising, steady, or falling. Just because some people start using a brand name for their new baby—Harley, Apple, Lexus, Porsche, Pepsi, Rolex, Marlboro, and Sony—isn't enough evidence of brand effectiveness. Nor is it enough to periodically measure brand recall, recognition, knowledge, or interest. To capture whether *customer perceived value* has risen or fallen, you need to establish some key determinants of brand equity and average their direction. One system is to use the Brand Asset Valuation (BAV) mentioned earlier, although Brand Dynamics and other systems are available.[3]

What Is the Digital Impact on Brand Building and Control?

The Digital Age is having a momentous impact on brand building and control. The rise of Facebook, Twitter, YouTube, LinkedIn, and other social media has greatly contributed to Customer Empowerment. Today's customers can do several new things that were not possible before the Digital Age:

- One person can send a Twitter message to one, two, many, or millions of others. Singer Lady GaGa's words and experiences are followed by 5 million people.

- Two or more persons can converse and chat on the PCs or tablets for an extended period on a low and even no-cost basis (thanks to Skype).

- Customers can use the Internet to look up consumer ratings of automobiles (J.D. Powers) and countless other products.

- Customers can see a product in a store, get the store price, and then use their cell phone to find out whether the product is cheaper somewhere else. As a result, electronic store retailer Best Buy is now more of a showroom than a salesroom.

All of this means that the seller's monologue message—that which advertising carries—is of diminishing persuasion in the buying process. Customers' brand preferences will be increasingly influenced by other customers and by easily available online information.

One major implication is that no company can consistently exaggerate its product benefits without inviting bad word of mouth. One angry customer of United Airlines developed a blog called "Untied Airlines," and invited other disappointed United customers to tell their stories to the world on his blog. *Any* bad company behavior has the potential to be broadcast. Brands no longer have the luxury of being free to disappoint their customers. But the possible result for consumers is wonderful: we may eventually live in a world where we can trust all companies to be good at keeping their promises.

Another major benefit of the Digital Age is that companies can invite their customers to improve the companies' products, and to participate in *co-creating* their offerings. This is, in a sense, like positioning their company to be a workshop where customers can help design what they want the company to make for them. The company can resort to *crowdsourcing*—using the Internet to invite people to contribute ideas—in their search for fresh ideas. For example, corn-based snack chip maker Doritos invited their customer enthusiasts to create advertising campaigns for Super Bowl 2012. Doritos launched a contest that they called "Crash the Super Bowl" whereby they invited consumers to create their own Doritos 30-second spot commercials. The contest received thousands of campaign ideas, and Doritos crowdsourced the general public after they were submitted and had them vote for their favorite of five finalists. Two brothers won a $1 million prize by finishing first in Ad Meter, and the user-generated ad won the top spot at the 21st *USA Today Super Bowl Ad Meter* defeating ads made by professional ad agencies. And the company enjoyed an additional benefit: the crowdsourcing approach created social-networking buzz as users viewed the entries online, recommended to friends, and posted links (called viral buzz). The vote was so close that the company decided to run two of the ads—and both commercials received high ratings during this Super Bowl.

Conclusion

There is no doubt that a strong brand makes it easier for you to grow your business. Developing the right name, logo, and slogan is the starting point. When the brand becomes really strong, it owns a word or phrase that the intended market comes to know well. Companies can then use this brand name to launch additional products within the category; in some cases, they can extend into other categories and occasionally, even other industries. But brands must take care not to stretch the name too far. They need to develop some system for discerning whether their brand equity is rising, steady, or falling. Be aware as well that a brand is likely to lose its freshness without innovation. The challenge is to find ways to recharge a brand with energized differentiation, or what we call *momentum*.

Questions

1. What *word* does your brand own? Write down words triggered by your brand name. Circle the favorable words, and put a square around the unfavorable words. Underline the words that are favorable but not widely known. Double underline the words that are unique to your company. What word or phrase would you like your brand to own?

2. Are you satisfied with your brand logo and brand slogan? Can you suggest a better logo and slogan? Does your company have a powerful visual identity?

3. Can you imagine extending or stretching your brand name into items you might introduce in other categories? Try to imagine some examples.

4. Where does your brand stand in the Brand Dynamics stages? What can you do to move it higher?

5. How do you determine whether your brand equity has risen, is steady, or has fallen?

6. John Gerzema and Ed Lebar published *The Brand Bubble: The Looming Brand Crisis and How to Avoid It* (Jossey-Bass, 2008). The authors say that some well-known brands have lost their freshness and at some point investors will realize this and sell their shares, depressing the company's share price. Is your brand still fresh? If not, what steps can you take to add momentum to your tired brand?

4 Grow by Innovating New Products, Services, and Experiences

Most innovations fail. And companies that don't innovate die.
—Henry Chesbrough

How much innovation has taken place in your organization in the past five years? Did you launch any new products or services? Were they major or minor? Did you invent a new way to run your business? Did you invent any new marketing techniques to sell to your market more effectively?

Apple would answer these questions positively, as would Samsung, Google, IBM, 3M, Caterpillar, and others. They all know that not to innovate is to stagnate. A company that does not innovate becomes stale to its customers, distributors, and suppliers—and it becomes stale inside, too. Its people feel unenthused.

We frequently hear the refrain, "Innovate or die." The dilemma inherent in this is that if we innovate, we will fail some or much of the time. Some companies understand this and persist in feeling that one great innovation success will pay for a number of innovation failures. The solution is in the numbers. Of course, the real solution is to innovate *smartly* and not fail.

We can learn a lot from the companies that have built innovation into their DNA and have established an organizational culture that encourages and rewards innovation. The 3M Company, a diversified multinational operating in 60 countries and producing innovative products in adhesives, abrasives, medical products, electronic circuits, optical film, and many other categories has developed procedures, roles, processes, incentives, and tools to make sure that employees innovate intelligently and balance risk and reward.

We need to recognize that being an innovator requires that you be both a creator (from your point of view) and a destroyer (from another company's point of view), because the losing company will mount a quick defense. It is important for the innovator to anticipate this defense. It doesn't make sense to innovate for the mass market if the defendant can keep the innovation from succeeding. For example, Procter & Gamble is rarely attacked. If P&G hears of the launch of a new cleaning powder, it simply cuts prices or loads products on the retailer's shelves so the innovator would hardly have a chance to get space and succeed.

Your organization needs to address the following major questions:

1. Why innovate?
2. How can you assess your company's level and quality of innovation?

3. How can you implant more innovative thinking within your company?

4. Where can you go to get good innovative ideas?

5. How can you formalize the innovation process?

6. How can your company use creativity tools to find better growth ideas?

7. How can you raise the money to fund the innovation work and pay for the launch?

Why Innovate?

Suppose that although your firm is performing well, you notice a great amount of change occurring in your markets, customers, competitors, suppliers, and distribution channels. Your competitors are going to China to manufacture their goods at a lower cost, or maybe Chinese competitors are entering your country. You see domestic competitors creating exciting new products, and you study rapid changes in technology; for instance, Research in Motion (RIM)'s BlackBerry handset is in serious trouble as Android technology and Apple's iPhone take over much of the handset market.

All of this makes you increasingly uncomfortable, because you have done nothing to formalize an innovation process in your company. Now you realize that failing to do so is putting your company at risk; for as Masahiro Fujita, president of Sony's System Technologies Laboratories said, "The risk of not innovating is greater than the risk of innovating." [1] You must begin to figure out how to encourage your employees and partners (distributors, retailers, suppliers)—as well as your customers—to think more innovatively.

How Can You Assess Your Company's Innovation Level and Quality?

Companies like Kellogg, Kraft, and Campbell's manage a great number of consumer products, so they are fully aware that they must work continuously on improvements and new ideas. Thus, the Campbell's soup division will watch for new trends and tastes in soup. They may add a creamy tomato soup offering in addition to regular tomato. They might even launch an asparagus-based soup if the idea tests positively.

Each new launch requires work in developing the new flavor, packaging, advertising, distribution, and pricing. Because Campbell's has done this before, they know how to develop and test the concept, and prepare everything for the launch. They have conducted the business analysis that's necessary to determine the breakeven point and the financial return on investment (ROI). To this extent, we could say that companies such as Campbell's have *routinized* innovation.

However, it's important to note here that we are talking about *incremental* and not *breakthrough innovation*. The latter involves higher risks—and hopefully high returns. This might be what would happen if Campbell's conceived of a brand new packaging system for soup or developed a rich-tasting soup with no calories. Campbell's is aware that their competitors have invented new ways of packaging soup. So while we would give Campbell's a good grade for incremental innovation, they aren't the best example of radical or breakthrough innovation.

Keep in mind as well that innovation is not limited to products. Campbell's has to build its business by thinking out of the box as well. How about following the Starbucks business model and opening a chain of nourishing *soup shops*? The atmosphere would be warm and friendly, the staff would be cheerful and helpful, and customers could sit as long as they want to enjoy "31 flavors of soup." Or Campbell's could move in a different direction and develop a vending machine that dispenses several different types of hot soup.

Achieving a breakthrough innovation is a fervent hope—but a rare event—for most companies. Such a transformation doesn't just involve a *design change* or using different *materials*. It often comes about via the invention of a new *platform*, such as the iPad or iTunes or a hybrid car. A new platform like this can bring many new products forward.

Kraft food's president Irene Rosenfeld, told her stakeholders that if the brand was to reach its growth and profit goals, it would need to dream up a new product or product platform that would bring in an additional billion dollars of annual revenue. Rosenfeld set up competitive teams to find a billion-dollar new idea. She might have been inspired by the pharmaceutical industry whose companies are always searching for a new billion-dollar blockbuster drug. An interesting question is whether it would have been more realistic to set up teams to search for new product ideas that would have the promise of yielding $250 million in annual revenue. There may be more ideas lying around that would deliver $250 million dollars than one that would deliver $1 billion in the food industry.

We have seen major business model breakthroughs in different industries thanks to the imagination of visionary business people. Exhibit 4.1 lists several of these.

Exhibit 4.1 Marketing Visionaries

- Anita Roddick   Body Shop
- Fred Smith   Federal Express
- Steve Jobs   Apple

(continued)

- Bill Gates   Microsoft
- Michael Dell   Dell Computer
- Ray Kroc   McDonald's
- Walt Disney   Disneyland, Walt Disney World
- Sam Walton   Walmart
- Tom Monaghan   Domino's Pizza
- Akio Morita   Sony
- Nicolas G. Hayek   Swatch Watch Company
- Gilbert Trigano   Club Mediterranee
- Ted Turner   CNN
- Frank Perdue   Perdue Chicken
- Richard Branson   Virgin
- Soichiro Honda   Honda
- Luciano Benetton   Benetton
- Charles Lazarus   Toys 'R' Us
- Les Wexner   Victoria's Secret
- Colonel Sanders   Kentucky Fried Chicken
- Ingvar Kamprad   IKEA
- Howard Schultz   Starbucks
- Charles Schwab   Charles Schwab
- Philip Knight   Nike
- Leonard Riggio   Barnes & Noble bookstores

All of these are visions of new products, services, experiences, or delivery systems—and notice as well that many of them involve old or mature industries. The Body Shop was a new way to retail skin care products in eco-friendly packaging and without animal testing. CNN was the first broadcast station to supply breaking news 24 hours a day, seven days a week. IKEA was the first furniture company to drastically bring down the cost of good furniture by introducing do-it-yourself (DIY) assembly and equipping their stores with restaurants and day care centers. Charles Schwab Corporation introduced discount brokerage in 1975, and became one of the world's largest discount brokers. It was the first brokerage to offer 24-hour quotation. Starbucks was a new way to sell an old product—coffee—by offering convenient meeting places and places for conducting business without rent. Each of these stories—about how one person imagined a new way to create fresh value for a target set of customers—is worth telling.

Let's briefly consider the last example: Leonard Riggio and the Barnes & Noble bookstores. Consider the traditional bookstore. You would enter it, meander past many books loaded on shelves, occasionally pull one out and examine it, often put it back, and move on. All the while, you'd be wishing there would be a place to sit, and finally you would get tired and leave the store without buying a single book.

Then in 1971, along came Leonard Riggio, who had run a successful mail order bookstore and subsequently a chain of college bookstores. Leonard decided to buy a New York City bookstore in decline called Barnes & Noble. He enlarged the store to carry 150,000 books, many times the size of a typical bookstore, and brought in a generous number of tables and chairs. He added a section carrying pastries and Starbucks coffee, and decided to keep the store open from 9 A.M. to 11 A.M., seven days a week. Additionally, he set up author and musical programs at night. Leonard didn't just run a bookstore; he reinvented the concept of a bookstore.

But there is another lesson to reinvention; namely, that it too might have a limited life cycle. All innovations eventually face disruptive technologies. Barnes & Noble is a palatial bricks-and-mortar retail model in an age of online book sales, dominated by Amazon and a disruptive eBooks technology. The brand has already lost the eBooks race to Amazon's Kindle and its margins continue to decline. Can it change its current business model to keep ahead of the times—or will it suffer the same fate of Borders and Blockbuster? Even such innovative retail systems such as IKEA, Walmart, and Toys 'R' Us always have to be on the alert for new disruptive innovations.

We must also pay attention to the growing number of marketing innovations. Consider the long list of marketing innovations in Exhibit 4.2.

Exhibit 4.2 Major Marketing Innovations—Old and New

- Mail order catalogs and direct mail
- Self-service in retail stores
- Credit cards, rebates, zero-interest financing
- Installment buying
- Frequency award programs
- Coupons
- Gift certificates
- Using a brand as a platform (Virgin)
- Customized products (The National Bicycle Industrial Company of Japan customizes each bike)
- Selling goods on a live TV program where customers call in to order
- Book of the Month Club, Fruit of the Month Club, and other forms of serial selling
- Hypermarkets carrying a wide range of products at low prices (Carrefour, Costco)

- Category killer stores focusing on one product category (Petsmart, Toys 'R' Us)
- Differentiated types of stores within same chain: Best Buy
- Exclusive lines of merchandise (Target, Michael Graves)
- Guarantees and warranties
- e-Commerce
- Groupon and other group-buying deals

Many of these have been around a long time; however, new marketing tools keep appearing. Groupon is the latest of these; the business model simply consists of offering a "coupon" a day, each time for a different local retailer or local experience. If more than a specified number of persons sign up for the offer, they will get the product or experience at a deep discount. Some discounts are not even contingent on how many people sign up. The key to Groupon is that it benefits the local retailers by linking people to businesses near where they live and work. Groupon has grown so fast that it issued an IPO three years after its inception, and its market cap was $4.78 billion as of July 2012.

Companies like Groupon force other companies to ask themselves: Have we innovated in the areas of products, service, experiences, ideas, distribution networks, and marketing incentives? Have we done so more than our major competitors? How successful have these innovations been?

And if you have shown little or no innovation, what is the stumbling block? In many cases, the answer is—your success. First, chances are that you're a successful incumbent in your industry and have invested a great deal of money in the current technology of producing your goods. You don't want to invest in any new technology that will cannibalize what you already have. This reluctance is called the Incumbent's Curse—the wish to avoid undertaking a preemptive cannibalization. Companies who have this fear tend to minimize the risk that someone will come along, and they end up cannibalizing *themselves*.

Secondly, the new technology may not prove to deliver the expected benefits. Or, it might take awhile to realize the benefits—and your profits will be lower in the meantime. This may alienate the members of your board, stockholders, employees, and customers, since you're putting your current high profits and dominant position at risk. You will need to both find a great new idea *and* have the leadership to convince the others that making a change is less risky than not making any change.

How Can You Implant More Innovative Thinking within Your Company?

What steps can you take to stimulate your employees and channel partners to think more innovatively?

The first step must be to have the CEO assert that innovation will be embraced as a major strategic element in the company's planned growth—an idea the CEO must sell to the Board and senior management. He may be able to convince them to invest this one time in a new technology. Of course, it will be much harder to convince them that continuous innovation—and *only* continuous innovation—will be the company's only hope to stay profitable in a rapidly changing world.

If the CEO is successful, the next step to take is to implant the new culture of innovation in the company. This goes beyond assigning a senior person to carry the title of Director of New Products, Director of Innovation, or Director of Business

Development. The company must install procedures, processes, and incentives to drive home this new behavior.

Companies such as Google, Apple, and the 3M Company use a variety of incentives—including money (in the way of bonuses, raises, promotions), perks such as time-off for personal research, deep discounts on Apple products, more holidays, recognition awards to innovation champions, idea fairs, and research competitions. Communications company Nokia inducts engineers who file for at least 10 patents into its Club 10, recognizing them each year in a formal awards ceremony hosted by the company's CEO.

Not only should innovative employees be well-rewarded, they also should *not* be penalized for failure. A company that penalizes its innovators for failure will discourage any further risk taking. Failure is an inevitable feature of the innovation process, and it's critical to learn from it. David Kelley, founder of the design firm IDEO, encourages employees to "Fail early and fail often." Even at a savvy company such as Procter & Gamble, as many as 80 percent of new products are disappointments.

Clearly, the Director of Innovation at any company should study the methods that various other companies have utilized to improve the creation, flow, and success of new ideas. The Director has to do more than cheerleading; she must study the way different successful companies have built an innovation mindset into their companies. Although there is no one right way, the Director of Innovation will benefit from seeing the different steps such companies have taken.

Here are four different paths that companies have taken to build innovative thinking into their company.[2]

1. Train an internal staff in creative techniques.

2. Recruit new employees with a more creative profile.

3. Give employees a periodic opportunity to deliver ideas to senior management.

4. Outsource creativity to other organizations.

Training People to Be Creative: Whirlpool Corporation   The first option, training people to be creative, is perfectly feasible—because contrary to what many people think, you *can* teach and develop creativity. The Whirlpool Corporation launched an effort in the year 2000 to stimulate greater innovation. The company selected 400 of its employees from a wide variety of departments to train in a number of "ideation" methods. They were to do their regular jobs, but with an eye to innovating. Since that time, Whirlpool has gone from a handful of product introductions per year to dozens—including the highly successful Gladiator line of new appliances, workbenches, and storage systems for the garage.

It is true that, as in sports, art, and other disciplines, there will be people who are more capable and who have more innate potential than others. However, you can still find the minimum levels of creativity required for innovation in a high percentage of the population—and in virtually all people with a higher education. What people need—in addition to an innovation process that clearly defines creativity's scope and role—are effective tools and techniques for generating ideas. Quality creativity techniques and idea generation tools can help people become more creative.

Bringing in Creative People into the Organization: Samsung
The second option is to bring people with a truly creative profile into the organization. A good example of this is Samsung

Electronics, which established the Value Innovation Program (VIP) Center in 1998. The center has different cross-functional teams working to improve Samsung's strategic offerings. One team works continuously on ways to improve Samsung's TV sets; another concentrates on cell phones. In 2003, the center completed 80 projects. Samsung also runs an annual Value Innovation conference and gives awards to the best innovations. The brand is now the world's biggest technology firm measured by sales.

And what is the profile of "creative" people? There's been much debate on the nature of such individuals. Many authors have analyzed the structure of the personality and psychology of the most creative minds in history. Exhibit 4.3 summarizes some of the major findings about creative people.

Exhibit 4.3 Summary of Major Findings about Creative People

When faced with the absence of creative people—or the need to identify them within our organization—we need to get an idea about what sort of profile to look for. How can you tell when someone has the potential to be a creator in the innovation process? Though the specifics can differ, this list will help you get a good idea of creative people's personal characteristics, qualities, and most common resources. It also includes information about the sensations and feelings they experience when they create, and how you can recognize a creative person. *(continued)*

Personal Characteristics

According to Gilda Waisburd, a specialist in creativity, the traits of creative people are as follows:[3]

- Flexible (they go beyond the obvious)
- Fluid (they generate many ideas about a problem)
- Elaborative (they expand the task in detail)
- Tolerant of ambiguity (they stand up well to conflict)
- Able to see the whole (they take a systemic approach)
- Inquiring (interest in many disciplines)
- Sensitive to the interests of others (they understand others' needs)
- Curious (interested in "playing" with things)
- Independent (they come up with ideas of their own)
- Reflective (they think about what they see and hear)
- Action-oriented (they go beyond thinking and the idea to act)
- Able to concentrate (they work in a consistent manner)
- Persistent (they don't give up easily)
- Committed (they get involved with things)
- Sense of humor (they are able to laugh and use humor to put things in perspective)

Personal Qualities

Frank Barron, Howard Gardner, Calvin Taylor, Robert Sternberg, E. Paul Torrance, and Robert Weisberg, all distinguished theorists on creativity, generally concur that creative people exhibit the following qualities:[4]

- Verbal fluency
- High IQ
- Imagination
- Ability to influence others' and one's environment
- Ability and propensity to take risks
- Interest in properly defining the problem to be solved

Common Resources of Creative People

- Use metaphors
- Use images
- Use logic
- Usually ask themselves the "why" in what they observe

Feeling

Creative people are passionate about what they do and do not become easily discouraged by difficulties. They exploit their own potential and energy, aware that their time is finite. For them, creativity is an experience that allows them to forget their past and future, and immerse themselves in a timeless present that puts them into a state of self-realization.

Manifestation

We can call a person "creative" when he displays the ability to come up with original combinations and syntheses. Creativity is manifested in the capacity to associate and combine ideas in new ways. There is also creativity in breaking an area down and seeing its components.

Setting Regular Occasions for Employees to Address Ideas to Senior Management: Shell Oil   This third option establishes an opportunity for employees to formally present their ideas to senior management. In 1996, Shell Oil launched a program to allocate $20 million to spend on rule-breaking ideas originating anywhere in the company. Once a year, senior management serves as an audience for a succession of employees who have volunteered to present an innovative idea. Each employee gives a 10-minute talk with PowerPoint slides, and then spends 15 minutes answering questions. Senior management then meets afterwards and chooses the best ideas. The ideas that receive a green light get an average of $100,000 and up to $600,000 for further refinement. In 1996, 4 teams out of 12 received 6-month funding for next-stage development. Of Shell's five largest growth successes in 1999, four started as ideas presented at earlier senior management meetings.

Some companies are flooded with ideas—so much that management doesn't have to set aside a special meeting for them. Toyota expects its whole company—management, engineers, clerks, and factory workers—to always be thinking about the customer's desires, convenience and safety. Toyota claims its employees submit two million ideas annually (about 35 suggestions per employee), over 85 percent of which they end up implementing. Toyota has been a source or user of many new manufacturing ideas such as total quality management (TQM) at a six sigma level, just-in-time production, improving every day in every way (kaizan), and lean manufacturing. As a result, Toyota not only helped themselves, but also countless other organizations who adopted these approaches and gained success from using them. For example, a Harvard case called Deaconess-Glover Hospital (A) describes the journey of this hospital to manage the hospital according to the tools and principles used in the Toyota Production System (TPS).[5]

Outsource Ideas: Apple   The fourth option is to outsource the creativity. Apple, as we well know, has a great reputation for creativity. But it also outsources help for specific steps. When designing its products, Apple works closely with the award-winning design firm IDEO. Although Apple could have carried on all of its design work internally, they knew that they wouldn't be able to reach IDEO's skill level. The driving key to Apple's iPhone and iPad success is application outsourcing. The brand never could have developed this rich landscape of functions internally.

Creativity is the engine of innovation, so the decision to outsource creativity should not be taken lightly. Which supplier should you choose? What level of confidentiality should you demand? Do you want a simple outsourcing contract, or should you be thinking about a long-term agreement? These are questions you must consider when outsourcing innovation consulting or creativity specialists.

You can also outsource in a collaborative manner, by establishing a network of external agents for ongoing idea generation. Procter & Gamble is known for its "Connect & Develop" approach, which replaces its traditional "Research & Develop" approach. The open innovation program leverages P&G's network of entrepreneurs and suppliers around the world to provide fresh and innovative product ideas. The program contributes around 35 percent of P&G's revenue. Some of the well-known products invented through Connect & Develop include Olay Regenerist, Swiffer Dusters, and the Crest SpinBrush. P&G established several outside networks of innovators to supply ideas to the company to develop in house. These networks include NineSigma, which links up companies with scientists at university, government, and private labs; YourEncore Inc., which connects retired scientists and engineers with businesses; and yet2.com Inc., an online marketplace for intellectual property.[6]

Where Can You Go to Get Good Innovative Ideas?

A business can adopt one of two views on how to get new ideas. The first holds that ideas will come to the company in the normal course of carrying out its activities. The company can ask its customers for suggestions or problems; employees will come up with inspired ideas; or perhaps an R&D lab will be working on some projects. Sales people will collect ideas as they visit their customers, and senior management will come up with concepts from reading the business press or management articles.

The other view holds that ideas don't just happen in this way; the company needs to install a formal system for *collecting and evaluating* new ideas. We favor this view. We remember an instance in which an employee told us about a brainstorm he had shared with his superior. His boss said that the idea was interesting, but given the risks, would probably be rejected by the company. The message was clear: "Don't waste your time on this idea and get back to work." This happens more often than we'd like to think. Many bosses kill good ideas because they want their employees to focus on their day-to-day tasks.

However, companies can benefit greatly from running two marketing departments: a *large tactical group* working on selling today's production and a *small strategic group* that is free to think about the next five years without becoming concerned with selling today's output. This small department has a single mission: think of what the market will look like three to five years from now, and use this information to figure out what opportunities this would open up for the company.

General Electric's large appliance group did this several years ago when they hired sociologist Nelson Foote to think about what "kitchens" might be like five years into the future. Would kitchens grow to occupy more or less space in new homes being built? Would people do more eating in the kitchen than in the dining room? Would we need larger refrigerators to accommodate the growing frozen food business? Will people eat at home more frequently, therefore necessitating more and larger dishwashing machines and refrigerators? Clearly there would be trends and countertrends but at least these questions would open up the mind of GE management to new opportunities and possibilities.

A company needs to take a wide view about where ideas can be generated. Exhibit 4.4 lists the major sources for new ideas from both external and internal sources.

Exhibit 4.4 Major Sources of New Ideas

Internal Sources	External Sources
Marketing research department	Customers
R&D personnel	Distributors
Sales people	Competitors
Employee suggestions	Suppliers
Business development department	Government and NGOs

We have already reviewed the ways in which companies can get ideas from internal sources. However, companies shouldn't make the mistake of relying solely—or too much—on receiving new ideas from internal people. This will lead to too much more of the same thinking and lead to largely incremental improvements at best. This is why companies must also take an outside-in view of needs and trends.

Customers as a Major Source of Ideas   Most companies have to improve their approach in involving customers in the new product development process. In the past, companies saw this as entirely *their* job. They would identify a need, create a solution, and then promote the solution to those customers with the need. At best, they might show a prototype of their solution to a sample of potential customers from whom they'd encourage feedback and suggestions. The company would finalize the product and measure the customer preference level and intention to buy at different prices—and then decide whether there would be a high enough ROI to go ahead.

All of this is changing nowadays. As such, this section will discuss three interrelated developments about learning from your customers: co-creation, lead user analysis, and crowd sourcing.

Co-Creation　Companies today are moving from just collecting customer reactions to actively *inviting* customers to participate in creating and developing new products. The traditional company-centric approach to product innovation is giving way to a world in which companies co-create products with consumers.[7] Brands typically do this by using new technologies and creating digital spaces where people can propose, rank, or improve on ideas. Another alternative is for the company to ask people to give their opinions and assessments of ideas that the company is considering developing. Co-creation usually attracts consumers and customers who are highly engaged with the brand or category, giving them the online (and offline) tools to express their ideas and help guide designers in developing prototypes. This can also be done via face-to-face work sessions, similar to focus group meetings, to which people from outside the company are invited.[8]

Co-creation is especially useful in business-to-business (B2B) and services markets, since these are places where direct contact with customers is essential and innovation requires a certain degree of coordination between the innovators and its target customers. Boeing works with each airline customer to customize the features that it wants. Co-creation sometimes takes place after a company has fully tested its own product internally (the alpha stage) and is satisfied. It then moves to the beta stage when the company chooses a few loyal customers to try out the product and supply further ideas for improvement.

Co-creation is equally effective in highly dynamic markets, exposed to shifting fashions and changes in customer preferences, as well as the continuous flow of new knowledge. Wikipedia is an indispensable collaborative network. Cisco and Microsoft provide many tools for collaborative product development. Here are three company examples:

1. **Harley-Davidson** has won an enthusiastic set of motorcycle fans who consider their Harley motorcycles to be an important part of their life. Their fans join various HOGs (Harley Owner Groups) to gather and ride together. Some fans know a great deal about how motorcycles are built; and some who live near Harley's headquarters in Milwaukee, Wisconsin, ask if they can hang around or work with the engineers. They don't want payment—only the fun and challenge of creating better motorcycles.

2. **Lego**, the Danish toy company, creates plastic toy building blocks and seeks to develop new structures that can be built with Lego blocks. The company invites young people to their website to build their own designs, and some hang around the company and learn from designers and even propose and work up new designs.

3. **Bush Boake Allen** (BBA), a global supplier of specialty flavors to companies like Nestlé, has built a tool kit that enables its customers to develop their own flavors, which BBA then manufactures.[9]

Co-creation can also be applied in what are known as customer advisory boards or panels. In these situations, the company maintains regular contact with a fixed sample of selected customers from whom it continually gathers information on new ideas and possibilities.

Lead User Analysis   Companies can learn a great deal by studying customers who make the most advanced use of the company's products—and who recognize the need for improvements before other customers do.[10] Eric von Hippel, professor of Technological Innovation at MIT, has trained companies to use Lead User Analysis—a process that allows them to spot and then bring "lead users" into the product design process. This system is based on the principle that if you work with innovative customers, they will ultimately come up with innovative product ideas. The technique requires that brands gather users or customers who are particularly innovative and have them identify problems and solutions. The main challenge lies in determining how to identify such customers and convince them to participate in such sessions. The 3M Company, one of the most innovative manufacturing companies in the world, launched 1200 new products in 2012. They have a program called "Submit Your Idea," encouraging people to submit ideas for assessment, development, and patent protection. 3M has a catalog of 55,000 products.

For an example of lead users casually inventing something new, consider how mountain bikes came into being. These bicycles developed as a result of youngsters taking their bikes to the top of a mountain and riding down. When the bikes broke, the youngsters began building more durable bikes and adding motorcycle brakes, improved suspension, and accessories. Companies then picked up on these self-made innovations.

Crowdsourcing   *Crowdsourcing* is used to describe an individual, group, or organization that decides to solicit ideas or solutions from others, usually the public, but also from specialty groups. The Internet has facilitated the use of crowdsourcing because the request for help or participation can be virally transmitted to countless people.

Companies are increasingly turning to crowdsourcing to invite people to help create content, software, or ads, often offering prize money or a moment of glory as an incentive.[11] Here are two company examples:

1. Fiat, the Italian auto company, developed the first crowdsourced car called the Fiat Mio.[12] The Fiat Mio project was launched in Brazil by inviting people around the world to submit ideas of what they would want in a futuristic concept car. More than 17,000 participants submitted more than 11,000 ideas. Fiat interpreted the ideas and began constructing the Mio in early 2010 and launched it at the São Paulo Auto Show in October 2010. More work is continuing today to improve the concept car.

2. Networking equipment company Cisco runs an external innovation competition for its I-Prize.[13] It invites teams outside the company to join Cisco in heading an emerging technology business. The winner receives a $250,000 signing bonus and up to $10 million in funding for the first two years. Cisco's rationale for the contest—which drew 1,200 entrants from 104 countries—is simple: "In many parts of the world, you have incredibly smart people with incredibly great ideas who have absolutely no access to capital to take a great idea and turn it into a business." Judges applied five main criteria: (1) Does it address a real pain point? (2) Will it appeal to a big enough market? (3) Is the timing right? (4) If we pursue the idea, will we be good at it? And (5) Can we

exploit the opportunity for the long term? The public judged the entries online, a forum where Cisco found the detailed comments even more useful than the actual votes. The winning entry in the first competition was a plan for a sensor-enabled smart-electricity grid. Crowdsourcing also gets customers to feel closer to and look more favorably towards the company and to create favorable word of mouth.[14]

Exhibit 4.5 summarizes seven ways companies can learn from customers how to improve their offerings.[15]

Exhibit 4.5 Seven Ways to Draw New Ideas from Your Customers

1. ***Observe how customers are using your product***.
   Medical device company Medtronic has salespeople and market researchers regularly observe spine surgeons who use their products and competitive products to learn how to improve their own.

2. ***Ask customers about their problems with your products***. Upon recognizing that consumers were frustrated that potato chips break and are difficult to save after opening the bag, Procter & Gamble designed Pringles to be uniform in size and encased in a protective tennis-ball-type can.

3. ***Ask customers about their dream products***. Ask your customers what they want your product to do—even if the ideal sounds impossible. One 70-year-old camera user told Minolta he would like the camera to make his subjects look better and not show their wrinkles and

aging. In response, Minolta produced a camera with two lenses—one for rendering softer images of older subjects.

4. *Use a customer advisory board to comment on your company's ideas*. Levi Strauss uses youth panels to discuss lifestyles, habits, values, and brand engagements, while Cisco runs customer forums to improve its offerings.

5. *Use websites for new ideas*. Companies can use specialized search engines such as Technorati and Daypop to find blogs and postings relevant to their businesses. P&G's site has "We're Listening" and "Share Your Thoughts" sections and "Advisory Feedback" sessions to gain advice and feedback from customers.

6. *Form a brand community of enthusiasts who discuss your product*. Sony engages in collaborative dialogues with consumers to co-develop Sony's PlayStation 2.

7. *Encourage or challenge your customers to change or improve your product*. Salesforce.com wants its users to develop and share new software applications using simple programming tools. LSI Logic Corporation, designer of semiconductors and software, provides customers with do-it-yourself toolkits to allow them to design their own specialized chips; and car maker BMW posted a toolkit on its website to let customers develop ideas using telematics and in-car online services.

Companies can also involve other channel partners in the innovation process. In a business-to-business market, collecting information from distributors and retailers and suppliers can provide more diverse insights and information.[16]

Competitors are another group that you want to watch closely, because they allow companies to uncover what customers like and dislike about competitors' products. Brands can buy their competitors' products, take them apart, and build better ones.

Technology Is Another Source of New Ideas   Your organization also needs to scan the new industries that hopefully create new products and new jobs. The new technologies include:

- Robotics
- Artificial intelligence
- Neuroscience
- Information technology
- Nanotechnology
- Biotechnology
- Bioengineering
- Digital and social media
- Energy science
- Food science
- Education technology

We hope that these sciences and technologies spawn new industries, products, and services that address human needs and wants. Exhibit 4.6 lists some of these potential areas.

*Exhibit 4.6 Emerging Industries, Products,
and Services Related to Different Areas
of Human Need*

Human-Centered Areas	New Industries and Products
Health	Genetic engineering, biotech, personalized medicine, DNA testing, distance medicine, immediately acting birth control pill, hospices, home care, cures for cancer, diabetes, kidney dysfunction, quick cures for smoking and drug addiction, outpatient clinics, endoscopic surgery, angioplasty
Education	Distance education, Internet self-learning, chartered schools
Entertainment	3D movies, holographic movies, virtual travel and experiences, digital photography and filming, YouTube
Safety	Food irradiation, clean air, clean water, biometrics, airport monitor machines, alarm systems
Physical body	New exercise machines, bioengineering of body parts
Work reduction	Robotic machines, artificial intelligence, personal transportation (Segways), fast trains, 3D printing, on-demand printing, nanotechnology, online retailing, mobile phones
Shelter	Factory-built homes, do-it-yourself homes
Military	Robotic soldiers, drones, unmanned aircraft
Energy	Solar engineering, windmills, nuclear energy, car batteries
Environment	Smokestacks, filtration systems

These promising areas of innovation are not just for large companies to cultivate; they also require individuals, small groups, and small- and medium-size businesses to make discoveries. Some of the aforementioned garage entrepreneurs are likely to develop new chemicals, materials, components, tools, chips, and other items that enable us to make progress toward larger breakthroughs. For example, Charles Goodyear invented vulcanized rubber in his wood shed in 1839.

Every organization must analyze which of these opportunities offer the most promise. Samsung Electronics, currently the world's biggest technology firm measured in sales, has drawn up its industry entry plans. According to *The Economist* magazine, Samsung plans to invest $20 billion in five fields—solar panels, energy-saving LED lighting, medical devices, biotech drugs, and batteries for electric cars—that have two crucial things in common: high growth as a result of new environmental rules (solar power, LED lights, and electric cars) or exploding demand in emerging markets (medical devices and drugs). Samsung would also benefit by allowing large-scale manufacturing and thus lower costs.[17]

Another outward-looking source of new technology ideas is to watch what is happening in developing economies. Here are two examples of technological innovation in China:

1. **Mobile ultrasonic diagnosis equipment**. China Mindray Company invented mobile ultrasonic imaging diagnosis equipment for Chinese countryside doctors. Unlike GE and Toshiba's large and expensive medical imaging equipment for large urban hospitals, Mindray's small and mobile equipment provided doctors in rural areas an affordable and usable medical diagnostic tool. This mobile equipment should be of interest to use in the rural areas of other developed economies.

2. **BYD's innovation on automobile battery**. Shenzhen-based automobile and battery manufacturer BYD has developed a

new battery technology that will reduce the electronic car battery recharge time dramatically compared with U.S. top three auto manufacturers. In 2008, Warren Buffett invested $250 million for 10 percent ownership of BYD.

Clearly there is a lot of innovation taking place in China, India, and other developing countries. The message here: Watch technological and social trends around the world for clues to pocket opportunities.

How Can You Formalize the Innovation Process?

Your company needs to establish a well-defined process for gathering ideas and for moving from an initial idea to a final product or service that you can launch with confidence.

The Stage-Gate Process Most companies use the eight-step "stage-gate" process shown in Exhibit 4.7.

Exhibit 4.7 The Eight Steps in the Stage-Gate Process

1. Idea generation

2. Idea screening

3. Concept development and testing

4. Marketing strategy development

5. Business analysis

6. Product development

7. Market testing

8. Commercialization

The innovation process begins with generating a lot of ideas and then screening them according to a set of criteria aimed to winnow out a few that merit further consideration. Companies then refine any deserving idea into a concept and test for its relevance and interest. They should also consider the marketing strategy that would be used in its launch. This allows them to prepare a business analysis of the cost, risk, and return that are likely to come from a successful launch of this product. If the results are positive, the company proceeds to develop the product prototype and actual product, conduct further market testing, and finally move to commercialize the product.[18]

The main idea is that the company must make a go/no-go decision at the end of each stage. As the product moves through the stages, those developing it learn a great deal of information. This information might favor continuing the project, or it might indicate that it should be terminated. A major error would occur if the company continues development all the way to launch, and it turns out to be a bad decision. Another would occur if the company discontinues developing the project at some stage when in fact it would have been highly successful.

Although the stage-gate scheme is linear, it does not mean that the user only moves forward. If the customer test of the product fails, the company can return to the earlier stage of product development and makes some changes. If the precommercialization business analysis is unsatisfactory, they might drop the project or change its marketing strategy to lead to a different estimate of return and risk.

The A-to-F Process of Innovation   Carrying out the new product development process requires different members of the company to play a set of roles. Each individual has certain skills and different relationships with the other role players. Professor

Fernando Trias de Bes of ESADE and Philip Kotler identified six roles that those involved must perform to manage the innovation process more skillfully.[19] The six roles are:

1. Activator

2. Browser

3. Creator

4. Developer

5. Executor

6. Facilitator

The *activator* is one who follows a lot of changes—technical, economic, social, or political—and senses some opportunities for the company. The *browser* will then research online any interesting opportunity and also interview others to get a deep picture of the facts that might affect the opportunity. A promising opportunity is passed to a *creator* team to work up and test a refined concept. If the test results are strong and positive, the concept is turned over to a *developer* team that can make and test a prototype, and—if positive—develop a production method. When the product has been produced and market tested, the marketing department turns it over to an *executor* team to launch the product. Throughout the process, there has been a *facilitator* who essentially funds the work and makes sure it progresses toward a completion date.

Exhibit 4.8 lists the skills carried by each of the six A-to-F role players in the innovation process. The exhibit also uses ovals to show the path that a particular project follows during its development. Notice that only a subset of skills was needed to carry out this project. It is even possible to determine this particular path's expense by estimating the hours and costs involved in each oval.[20]

Exhibit 4.8 The A-to-F Model Illustrated

A Activators	B Browsers	C Creators	D Developers	E Executors	F Facilitators
Scope of Innovation	Innovation Review	Synectics	Concept Definition	Experimentation	Subjective Assessment
Innovation Levels	Analysis of Adjacent Categories	Blue Ocean Strategy	Concept Test	Morphing	Test Levels
Focus of Innovation	Internal Consulting	Morphological Analysis	Pictures	KPI's Evolution	Delphi Method
Innovation Guideliness	Social Trend/ Social Classes	Laterral Marketing	Conjoint Analysis for Features Definition	Next Marginal Evolution	Nominal Group Techniques
Innovation Checklist	Market Trends	Attributes Listing	Drawings	Intensity on ATRs	Company-Wide Rating
	Buying Process	Scenario Analysis	Mock-Up	Area Testing	Philips 66
	Innovation Routes	Visits	Prototype	Market Testing	Six Sigma
	Technological Solutions	Co-Creation	Product Test	Product Testing	Cost-Benefit
	Design	Redefining Customer Value	Usage/Home Test		Demand Estimation
	Successful Strategies and Tactics/Learning from Errors	Brain Storming	Area Test		Profit & Loss
	Network Monitoring		Marketing Plan Guidelines		ROI Analysis
	Ethnographic		Patents		Scenario Building
	Geolocation				Market Test

How Can Your Company Use Creativity Tools to Find Better Growth Ideas?

We've discussed the many sources from which companies can collect ideas for new products and services. Which of these methods, specifically, are available to your company? Here, we examine the main creativity tools for creating ideas and concepts: *brainstorming, synectics, blue ocean strategy and business model innovation, morphological analysis, attributes listing, lateral marketing, visits and trips,* and *redefining customer value*. We will describe each technique along with an example and case studies.

Brainstorming   Alex Osborn developed the well-known technique called *brainstorming*. He would gather a group, give them a clear problem, and then encourage free-wheeling thinking that was aimed at generating a maximum number of ideas. He would not accept any criticism of these ideas during this stage. Osborn hoped that this process would provoke new combinations based on such operations as substitution, elimination, and combining/rearranging/transposing or exaggerating elements. After the brainstorming portion was finished, the group would criticize and eliminate most of the ideas until a few prize ones remained.

Synectics   Synectics is a problem-solving method in which the actual problem is not clearly stated to the group. It starts by someone encouraging the group to think about some other thing that will ultimately lead to revealing the actual problem in a fresh light.

The method was developed by George M. Prince and William J. Gordon in the 1960s, and involves four steps:

1. The basic idea is to define the problem or area in which we want to innovate, specifying some of its elements.
2. Then we think of two analogous situations, devices, natural phenomena, or anything else that relates to one or more elements of the problem.
3. Then we describe these phenomena.
4. Finally, we look for possible connections with the elements of our problem.

An example of this occurred when NASA wanted to design an airtight space suit. The participants weren't told this. They were told to think about "closing" something, and therefore came up with ideas like zippers, bird's nests, buttoning, gluing, and so on. As the process progressed, they received more information, like "This is about closing an article of clothing." Finally the group managed to end with a lot of ideas about closing a space suit.

Blue Ocean Strategy and Business Model Innovation　Blue Ocean is a strategy designed by W. Chan Kim and Renée Mauborgne to redefine an industry in which you are competing, thereby creating new oceans (new industries or markets) that are free of competition. Its aim is to move beyond the fragmented, hypercompetitive markets, saturated with competitors (called red oceans, in reference to the blood from the fierce fighting among competitors) in order to create new spaces where competition is irrelevant: in sum, temporary monopolies.

The main technique for creating blue oceans is to develop a *strategy canvas* that includes the main factors of competition, investment, and delivering value to customers in a given industry. Each factor is then analyzed, and acted upon through one of four possible actions:

1. **Reduce** (which factors should be reduced well below the industry standard?)
2. **Eliminate** (which factors that the industry takes for granted can be eliminated?)
3. **Raise** (which factors can be raised well above the industry standard?)
4. **Create** (which factors can be created because the industry has never offered them?)

These actions allow companies to completely redefine their offering, costs, and the value delivered to the customer. The most famous example of Blue Ocean strategy is the Cirque du Soleil. The defining factors of the traditional circus industry were ticket prices, star performers, animal shows, aisle concession sales, multiple show arenas, fun and humor, suspense and danger, and unique setting. By applying the four actions on each of the factors, this brand completely reinvented the circus.[21] Instead of having to pay a low price and sitting in a large tent on hard wooden chairs and watching horses, lions, and other animals doing tricks, the audience pays much more to sit in a first-class theater and watch a surreal performance of great movement and drama.

Blue Ocean strategy is ideal for developing new markets (new customers, needs, or situations) and business model innovation. It is business model innovation that has produced the likes of Starbucks, Amazon, IKEA, Tesco, and Dollar stores. It asserts that you must either invent a new model for your business—or be the victim of one.

Morphological Analysis   Created by Swiss astronomer Fritz Zwicky, morphological analysis aims to solve problems by analyzing and altering their component parts.[22] Let's look at an example. Step one requires us to define the objective: we want to make a better pencil. In step two, we analyze its component attributes: size, point, type of material, type of lead, color, accessories, and price. In step three, we list the options for each attribute, such as whether the pencil's color should be yellow or red. In step four, we choose an option for each attribute. Finally, in step five, we evaluate the above by asking: How would a low-price, large, wood, fine-point, nonadjustable black-lead pencil with eraser and sharpener look?

We can try, evaluate, and improve other options until we are satisfied with the final outcome. Morphological analysis is an ideal technique for innovating a physical product or service design. It is suitable for marginal innovations, product line extensions, incremental improvements, and finding niches within a given category. It generally leads to a more tactical than strategic innovation, although that depends on the problem at hand. Since its methodology is based on existing attributes and does not introduce new possibilities from outside the box, it also tends to produce less radical innovations.

Attributes Listing   This is a special type of morphological analysis that focuses solely on the attributes or traits of the product or service that you want to change. You list the characteristics of your product or service, and then increase or decrease the number. You check what the resulting product would be like, whether it might interest some of your potential customers, or boost the volume or rate of consumption among current ones.

For example, imagine that you want to launch a new sort of salad. After listing its qualities and characteristics (i.e., the ingredients), you play with the intensity of its properties: a mild salad, very easy to eat and digest that's rich in protein but low in sodium, salts, and phosphorus. Then you try out different possibilities until you hit on one or more with the potential to become a new concept.

Almost all product and service line extensions are done, directly or implicitly, using this technique: for example, sugar-free and caffeine-free soft drinks, vitamin-enriched products, and the like.

Lateral Marketing   Fernando Trias de Bes and Philip Kotler developed the concept of *lateral marketing*, which involves displacing a current product or service with an innovation that results from changing the need, situation, or customer. For example, gas stations used to consist of a small station and a set of gas pumps, along with an attendant who would fill the gas tank and collect the money. Today, most gas stations have an attendant who sits next to the cash register in a very large store that sells food, drinks, and sundry items to meet a variety of needs of the traveling customer, who has to fill her own tank. Today's gas stations make as much money from the food business as from the gas business.

How can one begin to imagine similar possible improvements or transformations in a goods or service business? The answer is usually called *thinking out of the box*. Imagine, for instance, a cereal company that is looking for something else to do with cereal besides always putting it in a box. Suppose cereal lovers report that they wish they could eat cereal on the run but don't want to load it in their pocket or in a plastic bag. The solution: Kellogg launches a brightly packaged chocolate candy bar whose chief ingredient is cereal.

Or imagine an educational group that wants to provide training for an MBA degree but doesn't own any real estate or buildings. How about providing online training over the Internet (distance learning) or having classes meet in a special train car on the $1^1/_2$ hour business commute of managers from Long Island to Manhattan?

In these cases, the question is how to meet a new need with a new situation—for maybe a different type of customer. Nestlé has used lateral marketing on several occasions. It led them to develop Green Coffee (on the analogy of the health properties— anti-oxidants—of green tea). It also propelled them to launch Nesquik Night—a powdered cocoa-based drink for kids that's meant to be consumed before bed rather than at breakfast. Lateral marketing is ideal for finding innovation routes with the aim of differentiating your offering from the competition.

Visits and Trips   This method consists of visiting locations with the idea that what we see may serve us as inspiration and stimulate the generation of new ideas. Marketers normally visit outlets or places where customers buy, consume, or use products and services. They may interview customers about the problems they encounter, and ask about their needs, aspirations, and desires in regard to new products. It is often especially stimulating to visit foreign countries to see how customers abroad relate to our product category in the search for new ideas.

Starbucks Corp. uses this technique. Michelle Gass, Starbucks' senior vice-president for category management, took her team to Paris, Düsseldorf, and London to visit local Starbucks and other restaurants to get a better sense of local cultures, behaviors, and fashions. "You come back just full of different ideas and different ways to think about things," says Gass.[23]

Redefining Customer Value   We can describe the process of redefining customer value as modifying the value that customers get out of our products and services. Every transaction consists of two elements: the customer's efforts (the price paid, the time spent informing oneself and making the purchase, the risk associated with the decision, etc.) and the product or service he receives in return. Value is the ratio of what the customer gets divided by his efforts. You can therefore increase customer value in two ways: (1) giving more (quality or quantity) for the same price; or (2) offering the same product for less total customer effort, facilitating one or more of the elements that go into the sum.

This theory's application is very simple. (1) We analyze customer value by asking: What do we deliver? What efforts do our customers have to make? (2) Once we know this, we play around with our options for increasing, reducing, or eliminating such efforts, in order to see if there is a final increase in the value to customers. (3) Once we have found a new combination, we connect and develop the idea for turning the new combination into a new product, service, or a business model.

For example, we can offer after-sales services—a high-profit item for the company. Or we can offer to replace a damaged or defective product with a new one, therefore giving the customer the choice. Furniture maker IKEA offers to save the customer money by shifting furniture assembly to the customer, or add a charge if IKEA does the assembly.

What Is the Role of Outside Entrepreneurs in Creating New Ideas and Jobs?   This far, we have mainly discussed the role of companies in developing and managing the innovation process. But nations cannot achieve high growth solely via the efforts of established companies. A great deal of economic growth comes from entrepreneurs who get bright ideas, work them out in their homes or garages (à la Steve Jobs, Bill Gates), and then look for funding from friends, relatives, angels, and eventually venture capital firms or banks.[24] What might start as an acorn in Steve Jobs' garage may end up as a giant fruit tree called Apple—now one of the highest capitalized companies in the world.

We know that entrepreneurs have accounted for more of the jobs created in the United States than have our large corporations in recent years. In fact, most corporations have cut the number of jobs as a result of automation, the Internet, and offshoring of business. Entrepreneurs, on the other hand, have *added* to the number of jobs. But we must do more to help them get the funding they need to start their companies.

Unfortunately, there is no easy way to identify and support promising entrepreneurs. One approach is to encourage universities to do a better job of helping faculty with ideas to get funding. Universities should have an interest in this because they are increasingly sharing the profits from university-related research. More corporations are outsourcing applied research to university research institutes for lower cost and more fresh outside perspective.

Another development is that the federal government is moving from basic science to translational R&D to drive applied innovation. But the impediment here is that the U.S. patent office is backed up at least 18–24 months. Help to bona fide entrepreneurs is very badly needed—and it can come from venture capital and private equity firms who are open to hearing new proposals. Any country seeking growth must recognize that it is entrepreneurs who provide the major hope for job creation. As such, our country needs to do what it can to encourage and support its local entrepreneurs.

A lot of promising entrepreneurial work is occurring in the developing world—especially in designing new tools and products that will lower costs. Consider the following developments in India:[25]

- The Jaipur Foot is a prosthetic foot made from rubber intended for below-the-knee amputees. It costs about $30—a fraction of the $10,000 cost of a similar Western prosthesis. The distributor is BMVSS, a nonprofit organization that fits about 16,000 patients per year in India and ships to thousands of patients worldwide.

- The Aravind Eye Care system, founded in 1976, is the world's largest provider of cataract surgery. It charges about 2 percent of what a cataract operation costs in developed countries and makes a profit despite the fact that it treats 60 percent of its patients for free.

- The Narayana Hrudayalaya cardiac care center, located in Bangalore, was started in 2001 and is now one of the world's largest providers of heart surgery and other forms of cardiac care. The center also serves telemedicine patients who received consultation and treatment at remote sites, and accesses specialists through satellite- and Internet-based telecommunications links.

- The cost of a Western-style hotel room in Bangalore is typically US $300 per night. But the modern indiOne hotel—where every room is equipped with an attached bathroom, LCD television, small refrigerator, coffeemaker, and a work area—charges only $20, and is very profitable.

We might imagine that the next stage would include these entrepreneurial organizations bringing their solutions to the developed world—thereby disrupting the high-cost structure in the West.

There are always opportunities for creating new products and services. While these opportunities might seem scarcer during recessions, the very onset of recession creates a search for new answers. Any company with a product or service should be able to think of ways to modify it, combine it, offer different sizes, add or subtract features or services, and price it differently. This is a time when companies need to think out of the box and create a new context for its offering. For instance—during the recent recession, Campbell's repositioned its soups to be seen as a food meal that costs less than solid foods. More companies need to move from *vertical* marketing, where Campbell's just makes more flavors of soup, to *lateral* marketing where Campbell's thinks of new uses and contexts for soup.[26]

We can cite countless examples of recontextualizing an offering. Nowadays, we can buy food at gas stations; we can do our banking in a supermarket; we can access a computer or take pictures with our cell phone; we can chew prescription gum to ingest certain medicines in our body; we can eat cereal in the form of a candy bar. We can't possibly believe that there *aren't* opportunities. We can only believe that some marketers lack the ability to visualize opportunities. Marketing doesn't have to fail in a low-growth economy; the only failures are marketers who lack imagination.

How Can You Raise the Money to Fund the Innovation Work and Pay for the Launch?

Of course, innovation requires attracting sufficient funds to cover the cost of developing and eventually launching a new product or service. For this, an established company usually goes to its bank. Raising capital for a publicly traded company is not difficult if it has creditworthiness. Large companies have financing options—such as unsecured (i.e., non-collateralized) debt—that aren't normally available to smaller businesses.

On the other hand, let's consider the financing problem that a young entrepreneur faces. She may have a great idea but finds it difficult today to attract funding. The banks have plenty of money, but they resist lending because of the great uncertainties in the economy—let alone the doubts they may have about the specific business proposal itself.

The young entrepreneur could first draw from savings, if she has any. Or if the entrepreneur has assets such as a home or investments, she can go for asset-based lending. It is likely that the entrepreneur would appeal to rich relatives, if there are any. Another option is to seek out an angel investor—someone with money who gets excited about someone else's idea and is willing to make an initial *angel* investment, which must be followed by further stage venture capital investments. All investors at each stage of the investment process want a share of the business in return for investing their capital. If the entrepreneur's idea takes off, the entrepreneur may launch an initial public offering (IPO) to cash in as Mark Zuckerberg of Facebook did, or leave it operating as a privately-owned company.

The main skill that the innovator needs is the skill of marketing the idea. Each possible capital source differs in its criteria for lending money. Many entrepreneurs are so excited by their innovation idea that they think that their enthusiasm would be sufficient to impress the capital source. However, while enthusiasm can be contagious, it's often not enough. We would advise young innovators to read *Attracting Investors: A Marketing Approach to Finding Funds for Your Business*.[27] One of the most exciting new sources of financing creative product start-ups is *crowdfunding*. Abe Fetterman and his wife Lisa Qiu raised $580,000 through online Kickstarter.com to launch their novel kitchen device. Angel-List is another crowdfunding source.

Conclusion

The world is changing too fast for companies to not change along with it. Organizations must move with the times—and this calls for developing a capacity to innovate. Clearly the risks when you innovate and don't innovate are both great. Most companies will not be capable of "relentless innovation." But even these companies need to come up with *some* changes for their products, processes, services, pricing, distribution, and promotion. They must train some of their employees not only to think out of the box—but also give them the scope to *try and even fail*. As we know, punishing failure is a sure way to kill innovation.

Questions

1. How innovative is your company compared to your competitors? Have you been hurt by competitor innovations? Why—and in what ways—were competitors able to out-innovate?

2. How should you go about bringing more innovative thinking into the company? Who should be in charge of leading this initiative? What milestones and measures of progress would you establish?

3. Where do you think you can find the best innovative ideas for your business? Are employees, customers, supply chain partners, competitors, or hired consultants some viable options?

4. Does your company have a formal process for generating and screening ideas and carrying a good idea into a final launched product? How might you improve this process?

5. How attractive are your innovations to investors?

5 Grow by International Expansion

Why did you rob banks? Well, that's easy to answer. That's where the money is.

—Willie Sutton

Most companies in a country start by selling something there. This is true of the local shoemaker, clothier, candy maker, and food producer. If the country is very large, businesses can grow and continue as essentially domestic producers. This happened in the United States, which grew for a century principally on its vast domestic market. In a small country, some producers might eventually try to make or sell something to one or more other countries. Certainly, if a business can make more money selling abroad than it can selling at home, it should seriously consider doing business in other countries. This can take two forms: (1) establishing your business abroad by foreign direct investment or (2) exporting your goods and services from your home market to international markets.

Engaging in Foreign Direct Investment

Most large American companies and many midsize and small firms have chosen the foreign investment route and have established foreign subsidiaries. The dominant purpose for starting operations abroad is to exploit domestic sales opportunities in new growing markets. Many emerging countries have large populations and high population growth rates of people who need shoes, clothing, furniture, and appliances among other things, as well as local manufacturers who need foreign machinery and equipment. These emerging countries need to improve their physical infrastructure in energy, water, roads, rail, and air transport. The West excels in agricultural technology, brands high technology, military technology, and in services like finance, insurance, law, health, higher education, and social services. U.S. and European companies in any of these industries must research the opportunities they can find in various emerging countries. For example, a European or U.S. insurance company can research the insurance markets in the ten countries making up the Association of Southeast Asian Nations (ASEAN)—Brunei, Cambodia, Indonesia, Laos, Malaysia, Myanmar, Philippines, Singapore, Thailand, Vietnam—in the hope of finding pockets of growth for different types of home, life, or commercial insurance.

Another reason to set up a foreign subsidiary is to create a low-cost base to produce goods to export to other countries from the foreign subsidiary base. Most of the content of foreign-based production comes from a variety of source countries and are assembled in a variety of destination countries. In this way, production has become truly globalized.

Foreign countries not only offer lower wage costs than the home country in terms of production; they also offer more versatility. For example, Apple does not produce its products in the United States for several reasons in addition to low-cost manufacture. Apple's executives believe the vast scale of overseas factories—as well as foreign workers' flexibility, diligence, and industrial skills—have outpaced their American counterparts. It takes 8,700 industrial engineers to oversee and guide the 200,000 assembly-line workers involved in manufacturing Apple's iPhones. The company's analysts forecast that it would take as long as nine months to find that many qualified engineers in the United States. In China, it takes 15 days. China sales also make up 12 percent of Apple's global revenues.

Many small and midsize U.S. businesses have opened subsidiaries in emerging markets. China, for example, has become the fifth-most-important investment destination for U.S. companies. U.S. foreign domestic investment to China reached $60.5 billion in 2010. These companies include electronics manufacturers, apparel makers, machinery manufacturers, and food producers, as well as chemical, plastic, metals, furniture, and sporting-goods producers. While we are familiar with Fortune 500 companies in China, like Nike, Boeing, GM, Gap, Dow, and DuPont, many small and medium-sized companies (SMs) have operations in China as well, like Zoll Medical and Masimo in medical equipment, Burnham in heating equipment, IPG in photonics, and many of *Forbes*'s America's Best Small Companies. And the low wage cost is not the only reason for this movement. Other factors include telecommunications, physical infrastructure, physical safety and amenities, transportation equipment and logistics, a high pool of university graduates, and access to local markets.

From the standpoint of foreign market sales, Walmart earns 20 percent of its $420 billion in revenues from overseas, while Ford earns 51 percent of its $134 billion from abroad. General Electric reaches 54 percent of revenues from other countries, and IBM exceeds this at 64 percent. Dow Chemical goes further at 67 percent; and Intel takes the cake at 85 percent.

What may surprise many Americans is that the very American-seeming company Amazon has reached 45 percent of its revenues overseas in Canada, Europe, Japan, China, and elsewhere. Great American agricultural companies like Cargill, ADM, and Bunge are worldwide. American MBA and EMBA programs from Harvard, Yale, Stanford, Kellogg, and other great universities are operating all over the world. What is even more telling is that foreign revenues often carry a far higher rate of profit than domestic sales.

Engaging in Export

Let's now turn to export as a method of business expansion. Some countries, such as Germany and Japan, are very export oriented. They make highly regarded products and services that other countries want to buy. The United States, on the other hand, is only modestly export oriented. In 2010, large companies of over 500 workers carried on 66.3 percent of U.S. exports—although they represent only 2.2 percent of all exporters.[1] The remaining 97.8 percent of U.S. exporters are smaller firms including manufacturers, wholesalers, mining companies, and agricultural firms. As of 2010, of the 1,307,303 firms with 10 or more employees, 293,000—or about 22 percent—were export firms.[2]

The United States and other low exporting countries need to encourage more of their companies to think, connect, and sell globally. If they don't, the United States will continue to import more than it exports—and face a mounting deficit and debt on foreign trade.

Global marketing is now a *necessity* in the Age of Globalization. Many emerging countries have developed full-blown multinational companies that are looking to come into the United States and Europe with lower prices. At one time, the South Korean companies of Samsung and Hyundai and the Chinese company Haier were small and struggling enterprises in developing countries. They are now major players on the world stage. Western multinational leaders must pay attention to multinationals from BRIC (Brazil, Russia, India, China) and other developing countries—countries in such fields as information technology, electronics, autos, beverages, skin care, and home appliances.

Among the fast growing emerging multinationals are Acer, Arcelik, Apollo Tires, Bharti Airtel, Bimbo, Bright Food, Geely, HTC, Haier, Huawei, LG, Lenovo, Modelo, MTS, Natura, SAB-Miller, SAIC Motor Corp., Tata Motors, Tata Tea, Ulker, and Vitra. These companies come with lower costs and lower prices, as well as high quality and modern technology.

Consider as one example that Taiwanese computer and electronics firms possess advantages in design, innovation, rapid response, and global market flexibility—advantages that Western multinationals cannot duplicate. The United States and Europe can no longer rest on their laurels and assume guaranteed leadership. In 2011, the President's Council of Advisors on Science and Technology indicated that the United States requires an innovation policy to counter U.S. leadership decline. The Council called for boosting technologies like optoelectronics (lighting and detector technology), new materials and composites, nanotechnology, robotics, lithium ion batteries, semiconductors, photovoltaics (converting solar radiation into electricity), industrial machinery, wireless communication equipment, and other advanced technology sectors. The United States ranks seventh behind Korea, Japan, Switzerland, Israel, and others in R&D investment as a percentage of GDP.

There are reasons to believe that the West—particularly the United States—will be able to increase exports substantially.[3] First, U.S. costs in manufacturing and energy are decreasing. U.S. manufacturing is growing less dependent on cheap labor as more American factories rely on artificial intelligence and automation to run them. U.S. energy costs are likely to decline with the discovery of vast deposits of natural gas and the progress being made through the process of "fracking," a method of releasing natural gas and oil from rock formations. Both of these developments will lower costs and make the country more competitive. As developing nations become wealthier, they will turn to buying more American exports—civilian aircraft, semiconductors, cars, pharmaceuticals, liquified natural gas, machinery and equipment, automobile accessories, and entertainment—not to mention famous global U.S. and European brands and luxury products.

The good news is that there have been vast improvements in global information, transportation, communication, and banking, all of which have helped to facilitate the growth in world trade. According to the World Trade Organization, world merchandise exports in 2011 were up 22 percent, rising from $12.5 trillion to $15.2 trillion in a single year, while world exports of commercial services rose 8 percent, from $3.4 trillion to $3.7 trillion.

In this chapter, we would like your company to consider the following questions:

1. Why go abroad?

2. Where is the most growth occurring in the world?

3. What capabilities are required to conduct foreign trade?

Let's dive in.

Why Go Abroad?

There is evidence all around us of international trade's impressive growth. You meet a German businessman in Egypt who is wearing an Armani suit, on his way to meet an English friend at a Japanese restaurant. At the end of the day, he makes a drink with Russian vodka and then settles in to watch an American soap opera on Egyptian TV. Products developed in one country—Gucci purses, Mont Blanc pens, McDonald's hamburgers, Japanese sushi, Chanel suits, German BMWs—are finding enthusiastic acceptance all over the world. The world is brand-crazy. Develop a strong brand, and you'll have the world at your feet.

Consider the following major reasons why you should think of going abroad:

- **You are being attacked by foreign firms in your country**, and you need to counteract them in their home market—at least to tie them up. British beverage company Schweppes entered the U.S. carbonated drinks market to offset Coca-Cola and Pepsi-Cola in their UK home market. They were eventually acquired by Coca-Cola.

- You have calculated that **you can earn higher profits abroad** than at home. Luxury goods have a higher margin in Asian markets than in U.S. and European markets. Chinese tourists shop for Gucci, Coach, Louis Vuitton, Burberry, and other luxury goods in New York, London, and Paris where the price is lower than in Shanghai and Beijing.

- By getting more customers from abroad, you can achieve scale economies that bring down your overall costs. The global passion for iPhone and iPads has brought down Apple's unit costs.

- You want to **reduce the risk of operating in only one country**, especially if things go sour there. With restrictions and tax disincentives in Western markets, tobacco companies are prospering in Asia, Africa, and Latin America.

- **Your customers have gone abroad**, and as their supplier, they expect you to do the same. Japanese automakers in China are bringing their suppliers with them.

While most companies can achieve clear advantages by going abroad, the many risks and costs tend to make them hesitant. Companies are naturally hesitant to enter into foreign trade, especially if there is enough business available in their own countries. The following are concerns that management might voice about entering foreign trade:

- **Do we know the language that's spoken in the other country?** U.S. companies favor entering other countries where English is spoken, such as Canada, UK, and even India over China.

- **Will the foreign buyer be able to pay in dollars**, or at least a widely traded currency?

- **Is it easy to get licenses to undertake trade and production** in the other country—or is the other country very bureaucratic, slow moving, and prejudiced against foreign firms? India, for example, is notorious for delaying licenses for foreign countries trying to enter their domestic market.

- **Is corruption a serious problem in that country?** U.S. firms have to comply with the provisions of the Federal Corrupt Practices Act passed in 1977, making it difficult to compete abroad against foreign firms that operate without this regulation.

- **Is the country economically and politically stable?** Greece and Spain are economically uncertain for investment. Nigeria is in constant turmoil for U.S. oil development investment. Companies worry about other countries' huge foreign indebtedness, political instability, entry requirements, corporate taxes, tariffs, and other trade barriers. Additional issues of concern are technological pirating, the high cost of adapting the brand's products and promotions, and a potentially poor understanding of the other country's business practices.

Clearly, making the decision to go abroad has both pros and cons. However, we would argue that we have little choice in terms of whether to go global or not; foreign companies will continue to come into our market and will force us to internationalize. In the 1970s and 1980s, Japan was a major threat to U.S. industries in consumer electronics, motorcycles, cars and trucks, copying machines, cameras, and watches. Starting in the 1980s, Korea became the country to fear in these areas as well as in the clothing, shoes, toys, furniture, and dozens of other industries. China followed as a threat in these areas in the 1990s. And most people are unaware that many firms thought to be American are really foreign companies—like Bantam Books (Italy), Baskin-Robbins Ice Cream (UK), Firestone Tires (Japan), and Crate and Barrel (Germany).

Where Is the Most Growth Occurring in the World?

As sales lag in the West, it makes sense for your company to start looking for opportunities in the fast-track growth countries. Let's assume that your company decides that its growth will best come from entering the markets of high-growth nations, such as the BRIC countries. Your company can turn to the IMF statistics showing the projected GDP growth rates for major regions (see Exhibit 5.1).[4]

*Exhibit 5.1 IMF Projected 2013 GDP Growth
Rates as Reported by Reuters, July 15, 2012*

- Global growth at 3.9 percent in 2013.
- Advanced economies only 1.9 percent in 2013.
- Emerging economies 5.9 percent in 2013.
- Eurozone to 0.7 percent.
- United Kingdom 1.4 percent in 2013.
- Italy, Spain, Portugal, and Greece negative growth (contraction).

We see three groups of nations here, according to projected 2013 GDP growth rates: (1) high growth (4.0 and above); (2) low growth (below 4.0 to zero); and (3) negative growth (−0.0 and below). Clearly, any company in the second or third group that wants growth should focus on finding growth opportunities in the first group. The first group is largely the BRIC countries and a few other large countries that are rapidly building a middle class. Their citizens have a strong desire for higher-value material possession and enhanced quality of life—and are acquiring the means to pay for these desired goods and services.

Consider a fact that we cited in an earlier chapter: China is building many new towns for its rapid urbanization. This is the best news possible for any company that sells cement, steel, furniture, architectural services, and other building inputs. China is dotted with new high-rise buildings under construction. Even if a company isn't able to enter the construction industry *in* China, it can consider entering one of the industries that will have to furnish and operate the buildings once they are completed. Every building needs a heating and cooling system, a water system, bathroom fixtures, kitchen appliances, and furniture for living rooms and bedrooms. Companies operating in these industries can make a fortune by cashing in on every new building that is completed. For example, UTC's Carrier heating and air conditioning division and Otis elevators do very well in China, and Kohler is a sanitary-ware leader.

China has done an incredible job of reducing its population of poor people and building a growing middle class. The members of this new class have the means and desire for fine dining with foreign wines, electronics, better-quality clothing, good-looking furniture, beauty shops, medical services, educational services, and so on. Pockets of opportunity are quite obviously more abundant in the fast-growing industries found in fast-growing countries.

Additionally, your company should consider entering other high-growth countries. Consider that the ASEAN region mentioned earlier of 10 Asian countries, has a good growth rate and more than 600 million consumers. These countries' citizens work hard, and they are eager to attain the standard of living of the West. Your company can work and establish a strong position in one or more countries in the ASEAN community. You should also look ahead at some fast-growing countries in Africa that are on the verge of take-off. South Africa and Ethiopia, for instance, have high growth rates; they are attracting foreign investment and buying more foreign-made products and services. Procter & Gamble has taken advantage of this growth by building a R200 million new plant in South Africa to produce disposable nappies.

Of course, we have to qualify this rush to enter faster-growing economies. Any company looking to expand globally needs to make five-year estimates of the costs and revenues associated with starting up in any country. Many countries will have already attracted your competitors; this means that you have to be sure that you can offer something better and different to attract customers.

Additionally, you have to decide which city or cities would be best to enter first. If you're considering China, should you start in Beijing, Shanghai, Guangzhou, Hong Kong, or another major Chinese city? Where are the best local pockets of potential growth? Your company needs to assess which micro-areas of opportunity fit to your company's offerings and capabilities best. For instance, Foxconn—a major producer of Apple's products—has moved operations from high-labor-cost Shenzhen on the east coast to Chengdu in the West and Zhengzhou in Central China.

What Capabilities Are Required to Conduct Foreign Trade?

No company should go abroad without first acquiring some employees who are especially skilled in foreign trade. Does your company have the right people to mount that effort? It would clearly be idiotic to send your chief marketing officer who has never been outside of the U.S. to set up trade in China. Aside from the fact that he has eaten in Chinese restaurants, he has little knowledge of China. He doesn't know the language, culture, or business practices. Therefore, the first rule for going abroad is to hire an experienced person or group who has done business in whatever countries you're entering, to help you evaluate the opportunities—and help you carry them out.

The hardest part is to evaluate how good these foreign experts are, since you don't personally know enough to *know* how good they are. If your early hires don't accomplish much, they will have plenty of reasons to give you. In this case, you may have to put this challenge or assignment in a second group's hands to see if they can do better. The following is a story that we like to tell about penetrating a foreign market.

The CEO of a U.S. shoe company sent a top salesman to a rural area in a small African country to develop the shoe market. He came back despondent and said, "They don't wear shoes. There is no market." The CEO, disappointed, decides to send another salesman to the same country. After one month, that salesman sends in a huge order for shoes. His message says: "The people here don't wear shoes. But they have many foot injuries. I contacted their tribal chief and gave him a pair of shoes. He liked them so much that he placed a huge order for all of his people to wear shoes. It was an easy sale, boss." This story clearly pinpoints the difference between a salesman and a marketer.

When you decide to enter a foreign market, you have to be prepared to do a lot of learning. Domestic companies that go international will initially lose a lot of money. They need to learn firsthand by undergoing the stages of indirect exports, direct exports, licensing, joint ventures, overseas sales branches, and overseas manufacturing branches. The purpose of going international is initially not profit, but *survival*. You cannot entrust international marketing to any manager who is not first rate. Companies will always be surprised by the international market, but good managers will be surprised less often and will handle surprises better. While many foreign companies start with expat managers, they soon replace them with Western-educated indigenous executives. These individuals first train in the headquarters country and then are deployed abroad for management, while expats are withdrawn.

Suppose you have spotted a very attractive marketing opportunity in a foreign country and your staff needs to design a business plan to capture it. Here are some of the major issues requiring decisive action:

- **Will the foreign buyers accept the current product/service, or will they require changes in the product or service features?** Food company Kraft built a cheese-making factory in China that failed because 90 percent of Han Chinese are lactose intolerant and dislike cheese. By contrast, China is a world-leading market for French wine.

- **Should the company build and operate its own production facility abroad or outsource, supervise, and monitor?** Apple has outsourced to Taiwan Foxconn, and Nike has a 100 percent outsourcing strategy.

- **Should the company set the price at a low level to accelerate early sales penetration, or at a high level to insure a good margin?** Marlboro cigarettes set a low foreign market entry price to compete with time-honored local brands. Marlboro entered the China market at a very low price compared to Chinese premium brands in order to gain market share and has had difficulty raising the price.

- **What distributors or agents should the company hire to make the product/service quickly available in that country?** Increasingly, eCommerce websites are the least expensive and most accessible path for distributing new domestic and foreign products.

- **What logistics should the company engage to ensure that the product arrives in time and in good condition to the destination?** Federal Express, UPS, and DHL dominate global air cargo. Sea cargo is fragmented. Pro Logistics is a global leader in warehousing and freight.

- **What insurance should the company purchase to cover the risk of these transactions?** Most global banks offer trade credit insurance.

- **What trade in services should the company include with the offer to the foreign buyer(s)?** Siemens, Bosch, GE, and Boeing are leaders in international trade financing where they work out long-term payment schemes to help customers pay for major equipment. Other services are cross-border trade service, direct service to cross-border consumers, cross-border commercial presence, and the cross-border presence of company personnel.

Those companies that succeed in international trade have the following characteristics:

- Company actively seeks profitable opportunities abroad and builds relationships. GE and Johnson & Johnson are two examples of the most aggressive global marketers.

- The International Vice President and team are very competent and experienced. Many global marketing teams' headquarters are becoming increasingly international.

- The international staff studies each market carefully and tailors its offerings and programs accordingly. Company staff uses international experts and continuously relies on independent commercial global industry studies and reports. Additionally, the international staff has developed a clear, innovative, data-driven, and well-reasoned marketing strategy for each country. Yet no company can internalize sufficient resources for international strategies. It needs *area* consultants.

- Headquarters has given each country staff adequate funds for achieving the agreed-upon objectives.

In order to succeed abroad, your company and employees will need skills in understanding another culture, forming alliances, and offering something that the customers really need and want—and cannot get elsewhere.

Conclusion

One of the most promising pathways to growth, especially for companies in a low-growth economy, is to scan for opportunities in higher-growth economies, particularly in the BRIC countries—but many others as well. Companies that are already engaging in foreign investment and exporting should give increased attention to these possibilities. Companies *not* involved in foreign trade should carefully examine the benefits and the barriers involved in selling and investing abroad. An increasing number of citizens in high-growth economies are moving into the middle class; more and more of them want appliances, furniture, better transportation, education, medical services, and other features of the good life. Companies in low-growth economies can supply many of these goods to the growing middle class abroad, not to mention to businesses and government groups in foreign countries. The barriers to doing business in foreign markets are, of course, substantial. They include language and cultural differences, regulations, politics, and even some protectionism barriers. Clearly, no firm should contemplate entering a foreign country before doing its homework and hiring the needed skilled and experienced people who have done this before, and giving them a generous budget to research the opportunities and propose projects that promise a high return in relation to the cost and risk.

Questions

1. Would you say that your company is sufficiently involved in foreign trade and foreign investment? What are you selling abroad and producing abroad? To what countries? Are your competitors even more involved in foreign trade?

2. Brainstorm a list of specific foreign trade and investment opportunities facing your company. Which opportunity would be the most promising? What changes would you need to make in your product, price, place, and promotion as well as your management structure if you pursued the opportunity? Why or why not will you undertake it?

3. Who in your company is responsible for managing and increasing your foreign trade and foreign investment? What improvements can you make to increase your foreign trade and investment effectiveness?

6 Grow by Mergers, Acquisitions, Alliances, and Joint Ventures

If you build up a business big enough, it's respectable.
—Will Rogers

Most companies strive to grow organically by winning more customer "votes"—usually as a result of offering better products, service, and customer care. The market serves as the forum for companies to prove themselves, since it's where customers compare competitors' offerings and make their decisions. Those companies with more insight into customer needs and preferences—and who utilize more innovative thinking—are likely to attain the growth that they seek.

Yet some companies also give thought to accelerating their growth and using their capital better by turning to acquisitions, mergers, strategic alliances, and joint ventures. Sometimes buying a competitor seems like a better solution than competing with it. Acquisitions are often essential for entry into related product categories. For example, BHP Billiton's acquisition of Petrohawk for $12.1 billion cash strengthens the mining giant's quest for natural gas assets. Companies frequently seek exclusive control of innovative components and systems that enhance their product or service line. Even more often, companies can gain exclusive or preferential accessibility to important distribution channels. The famous strategic alliance of Procter & Gamble and Walmart benefitted both companies: it gave brand status to Walmart, and granted P&G market access.

We discussed in Chapter 5 that going international is one way to grow. A company can seek to acquire or form alliances with foreign companies. But understand that each country has its own rules about acquisitions and alliances. Certain countries require a joint venture as a minimum condition for entering their markets. A company searching for a growth pathway must become familiar with mergers, acquisitions, strategic alliances, and joint ventures.

1. Why should a company ever consider acquiring, merging, allying, or joint venturing with other firms in pursuit of their growth objectives?

2. How can a company be sure that it has found the right company to acquire or with which to merge?

3. What major problems can occur in the process of acquiring and assimilating another company?

4. What about considering alliances and joint ventures as a way to grow?

Why Should a Company Ever Consider Acquiring, Merging, Allying, or Joint Venturing with Other Firms in Pursuit of Their Growth Objectives?

Let's be clear: no company can be successful as a lone cowboy. Organizations will always have to relate to other organizations in one way or another. They have to buy from suppliers, and sell to and through distributors. They must relate to a number of government agencies that regulate, tax, or send out bids. The selectivity and care with which a firm forms a relation with other firms will determine its success. General Motors, for example, works with different companies that supply engines, braking systems, seating systems, dashboard systems, and other car components. Ford Motor has its own set of partners. If one of these two competitors chooses and better manages its partners than the other, it is likely to outperform its competitor. The market leader owes as much of its leadership to its chosen partners as to itself.

Why Acquire or Merge?   Every company will occasionally consider whether to continue a market-based relationship with another company, or to actually take it over—or even consider a merger. An *acquisition* consists of taking over absolute ownership or a controlling share of another company, and either absorbing it or letting it operate on its own with some required changes. A *merger* involves two companies that decide to form a new legal entity, which is the merged company. Mergers generally take place between two equal companies; some examples are the successful merger of Exxon Mobil and JPMorgan Chase, and the troubled merger of Alcatel and Lucent. We prefer to use the word *acquisition* in most of the following discussion, but it will be relevant to mergers as well.

Any company is a part of a *supply chain* that may stretch all the way from raw materials, to semifinished materials, to finished products that have to be sold and moved by various distributors to final customers. At various times, the company may consider vertically integrating with one or more of its suppliers (backward integration) or distributors (forward integration). The main reasons to do this are to exert more control over supply or distribution and to reduce costs.

General Motors has made many acquisitions over its lifetime, buying both competitors and suppliers. In 2009, GM acquired several component companies of Delphi Automotive's worldwide steering business. This move gave GM more control of vital electronic supplies to fit its long-range plans. Acquiring a supplier, distributor, or even a competitor gives the company ownership power instead of just relying on market power. A major purpose is to exploit synergies. And acquisitions can also be reversed. After GM filed for Chapter 11 restructuring in 2009, Delphi bought back GM's shares in the company in 2011.

Here are specific reasons why a firm might want to acquire another firm:

- Increase its sales revenue, market share, or profitability by taking over a competitor (GM's acquisition of Cadillac, Pontiac, Chevrolet, Oldsmobile, and other auto brands).

- Enter a new business or market (Procter & Gamble's takeover of Gillette).

- Enter a new geographical area (Cadbury is very strong in UK and Commonwealth countries, where Kraft the acquirer, has a weak presence).

- Increase its ownership of supply inputs (in 2012, Sany—China's leader in construction equipment—acquired German concrete pump manufacturer Putzmeister to improve its product quality).

- Increase its efficiency by reducing job redundancies and operating costs (both steel companies Arcelor Mittal and cement maker Cemex have consolidated their industries worldwide for greater efficiency).

- Increase its economies of scale or scope (United Airlines' merger with Continental Airlines to become the world's largest airline).

- Enlarge its brand portfolio (Coca-Cola has grown by acquiring carbonated soft drink brands like Sprite, as well as juice brands like Tropicana and water brands such as Dasani).

- Increase its profits by opportunistically buying actual or potentially profitable companies (the holding company of Berkshire Hathaway under Warren Buffett is constantly seeking profit-making opportunities. It has acquired 100 percent ownership of over 40 companies in diverse industries, e.g., Acme Brick, Dairy Queen, Netjets, Helzberg Diamonds, etc.)

The desire to take over another company is not always considered a friendly move; in fact, we can distinguish between a *friendly takeover* and a *hostile takeover.* In a friendly takeover, the acquiring company notifies the target company's owners or board of directors that it would like to buy the company. If the board believes that selling the company would serve the stockholders' or owners' best interest, they will then negotiate an agreement.

In a hostile takeover, however, the board or owner is unwilling to sell the company. The acquirer then engages in a number of tactics to achieve the sale in spite of the target company's resistance. The acquirer can make a tender offer in public to pay a fixed price for the target company above the current market price. If the target company still resists, the acquiring firm can engage in a proxy fight to persuade enough shareholders (usually a simple majority) to vote in a new management that will approve the takeover. Alternatively, the acquiring company can quietly purchase enough stock in the open market to vote in a new management that is receptive to the takeover. The problem with a hostile takeover is that the acquirer doesn't get access to all the information about the target company—creating vulnerability to hidden risks. As such, the acquirer will find it harder to get bank loans because the bank doesn't want surprises. A few famous hostile takeovers include HP's hostile takeover of Compaq and Kraft's hostile takeover attempts to take over Cadbury, which eventually resulted in an agreed $21 billion sale.

Whether friendly or hostile, there are questions in any takeover. Is the price fair? What are the estimated costs? Can the acquirer afford the acquisition, raise the necessary money, reintegrate it, and handle the acquisition if the economy goes bad? Will the acquirer be able to keep the acquired firm's talent, clients, and suppliers? What are the technology risks? Will the acquired company be broken into parts to sell off?

How Successful Have Acquisitions Been?   One major expert in this area is Professor Michael Porter, who studied the 30-year record of major American corporate diversification efforts of 33 companies. Over 70 percent were acquisitions, 22 percent were start-ups, and 8 percent were joint ventures. Porter published his study in the May 1987 *Harvard Business Review*.[1] He reported, "The track record of corporate strategies has been dismal . . . most of them had divested far more acquisitions than they had kept. The corporate strategies of most companies have dissipated instead of created shareholder value." Porter concluded: "Managers should let shareholders do the diversifying."

Consultancy KPMG found even more disappointing results.[2] More than half the mergers destroyed shareholder value, fewer than one in six increased it, and a further third had made no discernible difference. And since mergers involve considerable trouble and expense, KPMG would count their failure rate of acquisitions at 5:6 (83 percent).

A few other notorious failures come to mind when discussing mergers and acquisitions. AT&T's 1991 purchase of NCR resulted in incredible losses for AT&T. Mattel's 1999 purchase of The Learning Company for $3.6 billion—only to have to sell it 16 months later for $430 million—was another feeble outcome. Daimler Benz merged with Chrysler in 1998, but the losses kept piling up—until Daimler finally sold it at a considerable loss in May 2007. Also in 2007, Microsoft purchased online advertising firm Quantive; however, they had to take a $6.2 billion goodwill write-down in 2012.

Why Do Many Acquisitions Go Sour?   Many explanations have been advanced for this—all of which should be in the bidder's mind before acting to acquire another company.

- **The acquirer feels a terrific high in the midst of a high-priced deal**. This fever is fanned by investment bankers, consultants, lawyers, and press agents. This has been called *testosterone poisoning*. Porter discusses this trend in his writing, and suspects that most deals have been done by bosses . . . who "confused company size with shareholder value."

- **The acquirer is focused more on the opportunities instead of the challenges during the courtship period**. When news leaks of the deal, key employees of the acquirer may see job cuts in the offing, and understandably they send out their resumes—and enough leave the firm to sink shareholder value. Those in the acquired firm see job cuts in the offing, and understandably they move forward based on these assumptions.

- **The acquired firm feels like a defeated army in an occupied land and stops performing as well as it had in the past**. Culture clashes occur between the two companies over

strategy, tactics, and organization. There is a loss of
motivation for employees in the acquired company.

- **It might seem to employees that they're working for two
  bosses**, the new one and the old one, and this confusion can't
  last too long. Even if it started as a "merger of equals," one
  eventually prevails over the other.

- **The acquiring company learns that it paid too much for
  the acquisition**. It may discover hidden liabilities in the
  acquired company. The acquired firm may have played off the
  different suitors in the effort to achieve the largest cash offer.
  There is evidence that this leads the bidders to overbid and
  "the winner loses by winning."[3]

Of course, we must be careful not to conclude that *all*
acquisitions fail. There are plenty examples of successful
acquisitions and mergers—some of which have been vital to the
company's future success. For instance, Google's acquisition of
Double Click made it the leader in search engines advertising
sales. We have to add to this Google's successful merger with
YouTube, and the mergers of Disney and Pixar, General
Dynamics and Anteon, and P&G and Gillette.

How Can a Company Be Sure That It Has Found the Right Company to Acquire or Merge?

Consider the following situation: China needs to acquire aircraft
for commercial purposes. It could buy planes from Boeing or
Airbus. Or it could decide to build its own aircraft, for which it
would need engines, wings, avionics, doors, wheels, and so on.
It would have to choose the best supplier of each component.
It might buy *from* a supplier, buy the supplier itself, or ally with
it. China's Aviation Industries Corporation is actively searching in

the United States, Europe, and Japan for new acquisitions that make specialized parts, components, systems, and equipment because existing suppliers will not sell their latest equipment to the Chinese for fear of re-engineering.

An acquiring company must perform due diligence that goes all the way from checking with the acquired firm's customers and suppliers, and making sure that the acquired firm is not carrying any hidden indebtedness, responsibilities, or commitments. Some uncertainty will always exist about a variety of matters: whether the acquired firm's managers and employees will stay with the new company and be easy to manage, and whether the acquired firm's customers will continue to work with the new management or switch their purchases to another firm. Many top Compaq engineers and managers left the company after HP acquired it.

What Major Problems Can Occur in the Process of Acquiring and Assimilating Another Company?

The two major issues in acquiring another company are legal and financial. The acquirer has to use or hire lawyers to conduct the proceedings involved in taking over the other firm's ownership. The first question is whether the government would allow this to happen. The government would want to be sure that the acquisition doesn't result in a serious reduction of competition in that industry. For example, in 2003, the U.S. Federal Trade Commission (FTC) challenged and prevented the merger between Dreyer's Grand Ice Cream, Inc. and Nestlé Holdings, Inc. The FTC held that this merger would reduce competition in the super-premium ice cream market from three firms to two, since Nestlé would now control 60 percent of the market. The FTC argued that this dominance would lead to anticompetitive effects—including less product variety, reduced choices, and higher prices for consumers.[4] Later that year Nestlé agreed to divest three of Dreyer's brands and some of Nestlé's distribution assets to settle the FTC anticompetition charge, and the merger went forward.

Clearly, it takes some time to determine whether the government would view a merger as anticompetitive. Once this matter is settled and the merger is permitted, then teams from the two companies have to undertake negotiations that can run weeks, months, or years. Each party will seek to gain the maximum advantage for its side—and both will need to compromise. Settling on the right price and payment terms is just one of the major challenges. In many cases, this is the point where the two can't agree and finally results in the news that the deal is off between the two companies.

The government might also object if a merger threatens national security. The U.S. Committee on Foreign Investment in the United States (CIFIUS) is an interagency committee that reviews the national security implications of foreign investments in U.S. companies or operations. In two notable cases, CIFIUS's concern about security issues forced Hutchinson Whampoa of Hong Kong to withdraw its bid for Global Crossing and induced Unocal's board to reject the $18.6 billion bid by China National Offshore Oil Corporation (CNOOC). Unocal was purchased by Chevron for $1 billion less.

Let's assume that an acquisition has gone through—because this is where the trouble usually begins. The acquiring firm faces two choices. The first one is to let the acquired firm continue to be managed by the former management team as if it had never been acquired. This is the general pattern of Chinese acquisitions of Western companies. Sany, for example, has agreed to keep the Putzmeister German factory operations, and German management is still in place after acquisition. This option will result in the smoothest transition for the acquired firm, because nothing has changed. As long as the acquired firm runs as expected and meets its goals, we can call the acquisition a success.

Choice two is where the acquiring company decides to change some things in the firm they've acquired. For instance, it might decide to reduce the number of employees, or to replace the former management. It might decide to rename the firm with the acquirer's name, as in the case of Delta's acquisition of Northwest Airlines. It might insist on changing the purchasing, inventory, marketing and sales, production, or other processes. Choice two is loaded with incendiary steps that might reduce the acquired company to a shadow or a ghost of its former self. This is the general pattern of Japanese acquisitions of foreign enterprises.

Yet as unpleasant and difficult as it may sound, we understand choice two. After all, the purpose of buying the supplier in the first place is to make it fit the acquiring company's needs. If the acquirer wasn't going to change anything, why bother buying the other firm? Why not just treat it as a supplier or form an alliance relationship? The acquiring company has clearly earned a right to reshape the firm it has purchased according to its purposes in buying it. The problems occur when these aren't made clear to the acquired company—which unfortunately often happens.

However, the acquiring firm itself can be considerably hurt if this reshaping ends disastrously. We might say that the acquiring firm has become riskier post-merger, which is what happened when Sears merged with Kmart. The new company, Sears Holdings, is doing poorly—so poorly, in fact, that the acquiring firm may end up with a higher risk of default. Suppose the acquisition was financed by the acquirer issuing higher debt, and cannot meet the necessary payments later because of an emerging down cycle. Or suppose the acquisition was driven by management seeking to improve its own compensation rather than for sounder motives.

What about Alliances and Joint Ventures as a Way to Grow?

If a company decides against growing its business through acquisition because of the risks, and it also decides against going on its own, it should consider two other options: forming a strategic alliance or a joint venture.[5]

Let's describe the differences between the two:

- **A strategic alliance** is more *informal* and describes two or more firms agreeing to do some business together.
- **A joint venture** is a *more formal agreement* between two companies to form a separate legal entity that has a certain objective, and usually a limited life.

Either of these can be formed between two domestic firms, or between a domestic and foreign firm. Of course, there are some distinct differences between the two approaches. This happened in the notorious case of the alliance of Pepsi with the Michael Jackson celebrity brand.

A Strategic Alliance between Two Domestic Companies

Consider the strategic alliance between Crayola products (owned by Binney and Smith) and creative art education company Abrakadoodle. Crayola makes the famous crayons that students use, while Abrakadoodle runs classes for students at schools or at other sites. Abrakadoodle agreed to order Crayola products for its operations, and use the Crayola trademark for advertising purposes. In turn, Crayola agreed to give Abrakadoodle discounts on Crayola products. This strategic alliance benefits both companies in encouraging children's artistic creativity.[6]

There are many instances of companies joining together in what is called a *co-branding program.*[7] This occurs when a single product or service is associated with a company other than the principal producer. The companies hope to capture synergy in the association of the two names. Here are additional examples:

- Procter & Gamble markets Gillette M3 Power shaving equipment (which requires batteries) and Duracell Batteries. In this case, P&G owns both companies.
- Citibank and American Airlines have a credit card joint venture.
- Betty Crocker's brownie mix includes Hershey's chocolate syrup.
- Dell Computers include a label that it uses Intel processors.

The underlying idea is that each company has a well-respected brand name and wants to borrow some of the other brand's aura, presumably to increase confidence in the product and therefore sales. Of course, companies must be careful about entering an alliance with a weaker brand, or one that might incur problems or a scandal later.

A Strategic Alliance between a Domestic and Foreign Company

As companies globalize, more and more firms are participating in foreign markets. A growing number of companies are using strategic alliances and joint ventures to enter foreign markets. In fact, many foreign governments require that the multinational firm find and form a joint venture with a local partner as a condition for entry—since the local partner better understands local business practices and the government wants technology transfer. The government may even insist on being included as one of the partners, primarily to prevent the joint venture from exploiting the country's resources, or securing the benefit of technology transfer.

Companies form alliances and joint ventures for many additional purposes. One company may join with other companies to get access to higher technology, capital, cheaper labor, certain materials, or marketing skills. There are many cooperative procurement alliances in hardware, furniture, apparel, appliances, and other consumer sectors. Cooperative procurement alliances are popular, because high-volume procurement drives down supplier prices. TCPN is one of the largest government purchasing cooperatives in all 50 U.S. states. True Value is a cooperative purchasing organization of independently owned hardware stores. Best Western, one of the largest hotel chains, is a purchasing and marketing cooperative of independently owned hotels and motels.

International marketing and technology alliances are also common. As an example, Advanced Micro Devices (AMD) formed an alliance with the Founder Group in China. Founder made and sold computers based on AMD's 64-bit microprocessors and gave it a supplier alternative to the more dominant option of Intel. AMD saw these alliances as a way to make a new start to its business in China. The reason that alliances and joint ventures are popular is because companies usually aren't likely to undertake high-risk projects unless they can find a partner to share the risk.

The alliance partners have to work out many details of course—specifically, on how they will share purchase quotas, revenues and profits, and handle the risk of loss or failure. It is very important to select the partner carefully; you want one who has goals that are compatible, even if they're different. The partners should also possess complementary skills. For instance, one may come with technical skills while the other may have access to scarce resources or capital, a strong brand name, or some other skill or resource that the partner lacks. Companies must carefully establish the terms and understandings to minimize conflict. The most important ingredient is that the partners trust each other.

Alliance partners may initially be equal in sharing their decision making; however, one partner tends to become more dominant over time. It is very important that the dominant partner be sensitive to the other partner(s) requirements for success.

Joint Ventures   A joint venture is a new entity between different companies to develop a new product, with mutual contribution to equity. The two organizations share revenues, expenses, and assets, and generally have a time limit with conditions for exiting the joint venture. The new entity can be for the purpose of completing one specific project, or simply aimed at continuing a business relationship. Since the cost of starting new projects is generally high, a joint venture allows both parties to share the project's burden—as well as the resulting profits.

Large companies have many joint ventures where they match their distinctive strengths with the core strength of another company. For example, Taiwan's Quanta Computer Inc., the world's largest notebook PC contract maker, formed a joint venture with 3M to produce touch modules, sensors, and electronic systems used in a variety of PC products. This was a new market for 3M Touch Systems Inc., which formerly focused on vertical markets like casino gaming, education, food services, digital signage, health care, retail point-of-sale, and the self-service sectors. One of the most successful contemporary joint ventures is between Shanghai Automotive Industries Corporation (SAIC) and General Motors. The Buick Regal is the top-selling sedan in

China, and SAIC has learned enough from GM to launch its own premium and luxury brands, the Roewe and MG.

Sometimes two companies form a joint venture when each has a weak market share, and both feel their combination of strength can make a market share breakthrough. Sony-Ericsson formed a joint venture to overcome its weak independent positions in the handset market. Sony sought to match its consumer electronics design expertise with Ericsson's technological leadership. However, the venture failed in this case—and after 12 unsuccessful years, Sony eventually bought out Ericcson. It is still struggling in the marketplace to this day.

Conclusion

Most companies grow organically on their own. But what if this kind of natural growth doesn't deliver enough growth to meet the company's financial and other objectives? Computer maker HP didn't achieve its growth only organically: it made 86 acquisitions between 1958 and December 2011. It also formed many alliances. So companies that want growth must think seriously about acquiring, merging, allying, or joint venturing with other companies.

But the record for success for these approaches—particularly through the acquisition route—is not impressive. In fact, the data shows that more than 50 percent of the acquisitions fail, and even more don't deliver on expectations. This has a lot to do with different motives for acquisition, not all of them honorable, and a lack of full knowledge of the acquired company before acquiring it—especially in the case of hostile takeovers.

Short of acquiring them, your company can still work closely with other companies by forming a strategic alliance or joint venture. Otherwise, you will only be relating to other companies through normal market dealings. The reason to form a strategic alliance or joint venture is to capture synergy, which happens when two firms may complement each other in skills such as technical, marketing, or financial. You should exercise care in choosing a partner, making sure that you spell out the terms and understandings in order to minimize the chance of conflict or misunderstanding.

Questions

1. If your firm has done any acquisitions, mergers, alliances, or joint ventures, how would you rate your record for success? What were the main reasons for any failures?

2. List a number of firms that you might conceivably think of acquiring. What would be the pros and cons for each firm?

3. List a number of firms with which you might conceivably form a strategic alliance, and the pros and cons for each.

4. List a number of firms with which you might conceivably form a joint venture, and the pros and cons for each.

5. Can you think of another firm whose brand name you would like to feature in addition to your own as a way of enhancing the level of interest and sales for your company?

7 Grow by Building an Outstanding Reputation for Social Responsibility

Be the change that you want to see in the world.

—Mahatma Gandhi

Most new companies start out by focusing their attention on developing a product or service that meets a need that no one else serves—or that they believe can meet this need better than other suppliers. If the company does this well, it will grow. Chances are that a company will *not* initially think of its social responsibilities, because it is engaged in more pressing daily struggles early on—like getting out production, meeting its payroll, and competing against formidable adversaries.

At some point in its growth, however, a charity, political party, or some other worthy cause will approach the company for contributions. The company will need to decide how to handle these requests—especially as their number and the amount requested grows. Initially, the company might make donations to satisfy the good opinion of those soliciting, not out of a real conviction that it has a responsibility to give something back to others in return for its good fortunes. At some point in the future, though, the company will realize the public goodwill it gains from donations and will target *one* cause that it truly cares about and try to make a real difference. Some companies may even get to the point of building corporate social responsibility into its very DNA—just as ice cream maker Ben & Jerry's or hiking boot and outdoor clothing vendor Timberland did.

Companies today are less free to ignore corporate social responsibility. More consumers and buyers are conversing with each other about the impact of products upon the environment and the health and well being of persons, families, and communities. Our current Information Age makes it easier for them to learn about any company's products, quality, technology, and social initiatives. As competition intensifies in an industry, most companies achieve parity with each other on their personal value to customers. They desperately search for ways to differentiate and to stand out as bigger, better, or different in some relevant way. One of the main differentiators left to companies is the degree to which the company seems to care about the state of the community and the world. Let's call this their *competitive margin of social value* to the customer.

Companies nowadays must ask themselves: *Are we simply a money-making engine for the moment? Or do we want to help create a better world and a higher standard of living for most people—and a greater opportunity for our own growth?*

We are essentially talking about a company's reputation, and what makes it attractive. There are a variety of elements the customers may care about: the quality of the company's products and services, whether the management is competent, whether the workers are well paid, whether the company is innovative, and whether its customer service is responsive. Customers want companies to be socially engaged, to contribute more to the community, to be concerned about environmental matters, and to manifest the customers' values. Chances are that more customers in the future will want companies to exhibit a more civic mindset.

In this chapter, we examine the following questions:

1. How can strong corporate social responsibility (CSR) contribute to company growth?

2. What are the major determinants of a company's reputation?

3. What major social areas can a company support?

4. How can the company communicate its values and social responsibility?

5. How can the company measure its CSR's impact on organizational sales and growth?

How Can Strong Corporate Social Responsibility Contribute to Company Growth?

Many years ago, companies thought that they were adding value to an economy by employing people to make good products and services. They added brand thinking later, which strengthened the company's appeal to customers. More recently, companies see their reputation as having to possess an additional layer drawing customer respect for the company (see Exhibit 7.1). As Professor Kash Rangan of Harvard observed: "It is no longer sufficient to compete on quality, price or product innovation alone," to which Dr. Joseph Plummer of the Advertising Research Foundation added: "The brand is what you buy. The corporate reputation is what you believe in and trust. It's not an either/or. You need both."

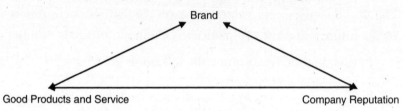

Exhibit 7.1 Three Platforms Contributing to Company Performance and Respect

Though unreported on most balance sheets, brand value and reputation still remain two of a company's most important assets in today's hypercompetitive globalized marketplace. In this Marketing 3.0 world, successful modern brands need to reach out not only to the customers' own hearts and minds, but also to their concern for the hearts and minds of others—and for the sustainability of the planet. We talk increasingly about companies striving to achieve a Triple Bottom Line: People, Planet, and Profits.

Now we have to ask: What benefits and growth come to companies that improve their reputation? We would list the following:

- The company is better able to attract and retain world-class talent.
- The company has created an additional level of customer-valued differentiation.
- The company may benefit by attracting more socially concerned suppliers and distributors who are aligned with the company's values.

- The company has mitigated its risk of being criticized or slandered.

- The company has attracted an additional class of customers who care about the planet. As wealth and education increase, customers are becoming increasingly aware that their own well-being is tied to the environment's sustainability and societal harmony.

Business for Social Responsibility is a leading nonprofit global organization that provides businesses with information, tools, training, and advisory services that help integrate corporate social responsibility into business operations and strategies. Their research and experience concludes that socially responsible companies have experienced a range of bottom-line benefits, including several of the following:

- Increased sales and market share
- Strengthened brand positioning
- Enhanced corporate image and clout
- Increased ability to attract, motivate, and retain employees
- Decreased operating costs
- Increased appeal to investors and financial analysts

Here is one interesting story of how a company wishing to grow its business also did some social good:

With 1,200 stores, PetSmart is North America's largest specialty retailer of pet products and services. But instead of selling dogs and cats, as many pet stores do, PetSmart decided to donate space for in-store adoption centers for homeless pets. Local animal welfare organizations maintain the highly visible in-store centers in coordination with PetSmart employees and keep 100 percent of their adoption fees. The adoption centers generate store traffic on a daily basis from consumers looking for a pet to add to their families. After all, every adopted pet needs pet food and accessories—and customers can immediately buy these at the same location.

Every adopted pet creates a new customer for PetSmart. More than 403,000 pets were adopted in PetSmart stores in 2010. Sales revenue far exceeds the estimated $13 million of contributed real estate floor space. In this way, the company has grown its business revenue by doing good works—and has exhibited real out-of-the box thinking. The company is earning more revenues at a lower cost by facilitating nonprofit adoption than they could ever have made by selling pets and pet products and accessories. And PetSmart helped save the lives of more than 5 million animals between 1994 and 2012.

What Are the Major Determinants of a Company's Reputation?

Many people know that reputations take a long time to build and a short time to damage. Several companies are known and admired for their contributions to environmental sustainability and worker welfare. Toyota, for instance, received well deserved kudos for introducing its hybrid Prius automobile, which gets 50 miles per gallon. GE won praise for its Ecomagination effort to make money by solving environmental problems, having launched green industries such as wind power and solar panels. Starbucks is admired for using purchasing practices that help coffee farmers achieve a decent income, and Reebok was the first in its industry to adopt standards for fair treatment of workers.

On the other hand, there are certainly enough examples of companies that draw criticism for their indifference. Walmart periodically gets into the news when its employees loudly complain about low pay and the lack of benefits. Nike had a public relations disaster when it was discovered that its overseas manufacturers were using child labor.

One needs to look at five questions when rating a company's overall reputation:

1. Does the company produce good or excellent-quality products and services? If the answer is no, there's no need to even ask any of the other questions.

2. Does the company show good profits over the long term? If not, people aren't likely to trust it.

3. Does the company have good management or even visionary management, or are its leaders asleep at the wheel?

4. Does the company have dedicated employees, suppliers, and distributors? This will come across in good teamwork and satisfied stakeholders.

5. Does the company exhibit social responsibility in a meaningful way? This last question adds another level to the company's overall reputation.

A company can convey its stand on social responsibility in the way that it is organized. For instance, most are organized as for-profit companies that serve the interests of the owners and investors. There are four alternative forms of organization.

1. One is the *employee-owned company*, which makes the point that the employees are the main beneficiary along with the company's customers. W. W. Norton & Company, America's largest independent book publishing company, is employee-owned, as is Huawei, China's second-largest supplier of mobile telecommunications infrastructure equipment in the world.

2. A second is the *mutual company*, as found in the insurance industry where the customers are the main beneficiary of

company performance. Mutual of Omaha and Northwestern Mutual are leading mutual organizations in the insurance industry. The Vanguard Group and TIAA-CREF (Teachers Insurance and Annuity Association—College Retirement Equities Fund) are leading mutual financial institutions in the United States.

3. A third is the *cooperative*, in which a board representing the members runs the organization in the interests of the members, who also earn points to the extent they make their purchases from the cooperative. Ocean Spray and Land O' Lakes in the United States are among thousands of cooperatives in Europe, India, and other regions of the world.

4. A fourth is the *benefit corporation*, which is a company run for profit but that takes into account the social, environmental, and community impact of its activities. The benefit corporation is midway between a for-profit company and a nonprofit charity. It is very similar to a social entrepreneur organization that is trying to reconcile making money and doing good. A good example is Patagonia, whose CEO Yvon Chouinard expresses this purpose of making money and doing good publicly. The company is putting sustainability ahead of profit and asking consumers to 'buy less'. All of these organization forms suggest something more than running a strict money-making machine for owners and investors.

What Are the Major Social Areas That a Company Can Support?

The International Organization for Standardization (ISO) has launched guidelines for social responsibility that cover the following areas: environment, human rights, labor practices, consumer issues, organizational governance, fair business practices, and community involvement/society development.

Consumers were asked what they thought that companies should be responsible for. Among the highest-rated responses were:

- Ensuring health and safety of products
- Not harming the environment
- Treating employees fairly

As an example of a company that takes social responsibility seriously, consider South Korea's Samsung, whose programs include the following:

- Education: Samsung Child Care Centers, Scholarships Program, Human Resources Development Center
- Environment: Samsung Global Environmental Research Center, adopt a river/mountain
- Sports sponsorships: Olympics
- Children: 4 Seasons of Hope, Pets as Therapy, Samsung's Children Museum
- Health: Samsung Guide Dog School, Eyesight Recovery
- Arts & Culture: Bolshoi Ballet, Hermitage Museum, Ho-Am Art Museum, Innovative Design Lab, Samsung Art & Design Institute

The authors of the book *Good Works!* describe six social initiative categories.[1] Your company should review these categories and determine in which ones it wants to express its social responsibility.

1. **Cause Promotions**: This occurs when a company decides to provide funds, in-kind contributions, or other corporate resources to help promote increased awareness and concern about a social cause; or to support fundraising, participation,

or volunteer recruitment for a cause. The company may manage the promotion on its own (e.g., The Body Shop successfully promoting a ban in the European Union on the use of animal testing to develop cosmetics); may be a major partner in an effort (e.g., Amgen-Pfizer sponsoring the Arthritis Foundation's fundraising walk); or it may be one of several sponsors (e.g., Keep America Beautiful 2011: Major sponsors for the Great American Cleanup included The Dow Chemical Company, Lowe's, Pepsi-Cola, Solo Cup Company, Scotts, Glade, and Nestlé).

2. **Cause-Related Marketing**: In this scenario, the company promises to contribute money or in-kind donations to a specific charity depending on the level of customer purchases of a specific product during a specific period. The company might partner with a nonprofit organization (e.g., Kraft Foods donates meals to Feeding America when consumers redeem coupons). This is a win-win-win (company/customer/charity) opportunity, because consumers get a discount on the product and are also contributing to a favorite charity.

3. **Corporate Social Marketing**: In this case, a company decides to support a behavior-change campaign to improve public health, safety, the environment, or community well-being. This differs from *cause promotions* because it focuses on producing an actual change in behavior, not just promoting more awareness of a cause. The company may implement a behavior change campaign on its own (e.g., Allstate encouraging teens to sign a pledge not to text and drive) or involve partners in public sector agencies (e.g., Home Depot and a utility service promoting water conservation tips) and/or nonprofit organizations (e.g., Pampers and the SIDS Foundation educating caretakers to place infants on their back when they go to sleep).

4. **Corporate Philanthropy**: This describes what happens when a company makes a direct contribution to a charity or cause, most often in the form of cash grants, donations, and/or in-kind services. This is the most traditional of all corporate social initiatives, but a growing number of companies are now moving to a more strategic approach; that is, they're choosing a focus and tying philanthropic activities more closely to the company's business operations, goals, and objectives. An example is Nestlé's contributions to the Nutritional Science Foundation. The advent of social media has made it easier for some companies to invite their customers to participate in determining which nonprofits should receive contributions (e.g., the JP Morgan Chase community giving program allocated $3 million in 2011 for 100 charities selected by Facebook users).

5. **Workforce Volunteering**: A company may encourage and support its employees, retail partners, and/or franchise members to *volunteer* at local community organizations and causes. They may do it as a standalone effort (e.g., employees of a high-tech company tutoring youth in middle schools on computer skills) or be in partnership with a nonprofit organization (e.g., AT&T working with the American Red Cross to supply phones for disaster relief efforts).

6. **Socially Responsible Business Practices**: This is when a company invests in social causes to improve community well-being and protect the environment. The company may conceive and implement the initiative (e.g., DuPont deciding to slash energy use and greenhouse gas emissions), or it may partner with others (e.g., Whole Foods Market working with the United Kingdom's Department of the Environment, Food, and Rural Affairs to increase purchasing of sustainable fish species).

How Can the Company Communicate Its Values and Social Responsibility?

What if your company is very active in supporting worthwhile causes—but few citizens know about it? Can your company depend on natural word of mouth from the gift's appreciative recipients, or do you need to take steps to amplify this acknowledgment? And if the latter scenario is the case—what channels can you use, and what are the risks of a company tooting its own horn?

Companies operating in today's Information Age have a great many channels at their fingertips for conveying a message to the general public or to specific target audiences. The company has available both traditional mass media platforms (newspapers, magazines, radio, TV, and billboards) as well as digital platforms and social media (Facebook, Twitter, YouTube, and others).

Let's consider a real example of what a company might do. Many people do not know that Walmart has an aggressive program in which they double the fuel efficiency of their own trucks and their suppliers' trucks. Recall that we mentioned earlier that Walmart is in the process of replacing its current truck fleet with fuel-efficient vehicles that will reduce emissions and costs, and are putting pressure on suppliers to buy more fuel-efficient trucks as well. This would lower the supplier's operating costs, lower Walmart's cost, and reduce the amount of air pollution.

Most people would applaud Walmart's action on behalf of a better environment. If Walmart believes that more members of the public should know about their initiative, the company's marketers or public relations people should prepare a long list of possible communications—including the following:

1. Take out full-page ads in newspapers and magazines describing this initiative.

2. Insert this information in a 30-second commercial about Walmart.

3. Develop a billboard ad about this initiative.

4. Describe this initiative on Walmart's web page.

5. Describe this initiative on Walmart's Facebook page.

6. Spread the word via Twitter.

7. Prepare a five-minute video to be shown on YouTube.

Clearly, Walmart has a large number of possibilities. You can imagine that Walmart management will debate these internally; they may decide to do nothing or to develop a specific plan to promote their good citizenship.

How Can the Company Measure Its CSR Impact on Company Sales and Growth?

Most companies should be satisfied with the knowledge that they have contributed to the social good—even if they cannot measure the impact of these initiatives on their sales and profits. After all, the initiatives have potentially reduced pollution, helped poor people, advanced the level of education, and done countless other good things. It's highly unlikely that the company's good works have *hurt* its sales and growth. Yet some companies may want to estimate by how *much* more sales have grown than they would if the company hadn't made any social responsibility contribution at all.

One way to do this is as follows: let's say that the company identifies two similar communities. It runs a strong social responsibility program in one community, and not in the other. It could compare the sales in the two communities. If there is no difference, and other things are equal, it would judge that the investment in CSR did not elevate sales. Short of this experimental design, the company might simply interview persons in the community that received the CSR to determine whether they remember being aware or more interested, or even whether they were led to purchase more of the company's products as a result of the CSR. But even if the return on this investment is zero or cannot be measured, the company deserves credit for making the social contribution.

We are witnessing a time during which more business leaders approach social responsibility as a moral commitment, rather than as opportunism or responding to social pressure. Consider the genuine commitments of the Bill Gates Foundation and Warren Buffett's pledges. Wealthy corporate leaders are becoming more decisively committed to social improvement and are organizing collectively to give billions. It seems that moral leaders feel compelled to share their wealth differently than they had in the past. They feel that a greater part of corporate and personal wealth should go to society and a bit less to shareholders and family enrichment. The fact that some, like Warren Buffett, are asking to be taxed *more* is also worth noting—as is the fact that Buffett is still actively running his fund and therefore subject to investors' concerns. Unlike Bill Gates, who is effectively retired, Buffett is driving his views as an active corporate leader morally committed to social leadership.

Conclusion

The International Organization for Standardization (ISO) has launched guidelines for social responsibility that cover the following areas: environment, human rights, labor practices, consumer issues, organizational governance, fair business practices, community involvement, and social development. Has your company connected with any of these social responsibility areas?

We believe that another pathway to growth is for a company to establish a reputation for caring about its stakeholders, the community and society at large, and society's future. The company can attract and keep customers who care about today's problems and the future for their children and grandchildren. Employees in a socially responsible company are likely to feel that they are part of something larger than a money-making machine. Many investors, suppliers, and distributors will react positively to the company's social responsibility initiatives.

We can remember a time when the only company that could truly claim that it made the safest car—Volvo—enjoyed two or more decades of prosperity because it cared about a basic human concern. However, Volvo lost its uniqueness when other auto companies improved their cars' safety. But it still pays for a company to try to solve some human problem. After all—isn't it better for all car brands to care about safety—instead of just one? In our rapidly growing, technological, machine-like world—one that's constantly worried about poverty, climate change, pollution, and water shortages—there is a growing interest in finding, designing, and nurturing a more human landscape where people have the opportunity to live a fuller and more satisfying life. Companies need to reach out and share the concerns that are preoccupying people's minds and hearts.

Each company has to find its own way to express sharing these concerns. Companies such as Timberland, Patagonia, Body Shop, and Starbucks all manifest their caring in different ways. Caring is not so much a matter of how much one gives, but how that social care is manifest in the business model, offerings, and business practices.

Questions

1. What efforts has your company given to social responsibility? Is your giving miscellaneous or focused on a central theme? Are you engaging in more or less social responsibility activities than your competitors?

2. Generate a list of three or more focused issues that your company might care about. Discuss the pros and cons of adopting each possible focused issue. Which would make the most sense for your type of company to support?

3. How do you manifest your social concerns in your business organization, products or services, and business practices?

4. Have your social responsibility efforts been effective in attracting new customers or increasing current customers' commitment? Have these efforts increased employee commitment? What effect have your social responsibility efforts had on your suppliers and distributors?

5. Does the public know about your level of commitment to social responsibility? If not, would you want them to know more—and how would you go about informing them?

8 Grow by Partnering with Government and NGOs

Time spent on reconnaissance is seldom wasted.

—Sun Tzu

Every nation's gross domestic product is made up of three components: consumer, business, and government spending. The percentage that the government spends as a ratio to GDP varies considerably among nations, from those where government plays a small role, like Guatemala (13.7 percent) and Cambodia (13.9 percent) to those where government plays a major role. European countries like France, Sweden, and Belgium are in the 50 to 53 percent range. China, Russia, India, and the United States are below 40 percent. At the extreme high end of the government spending scale are Zimbabwe, which spends 97.8 percent, and Cuba, which spends 78 percent of GDP.

We can highlight and better understand the issues and opportunities connected with government spending by examining our own government's spending. In 2010, total U.S. government spending was about 40 percent of GDP. Of this 40 percent, the federal government spends 20 percent, the states spend

10 percent, and local government spends another 10 percent. The money goes towards defense, education, health care, welfare, transportation, pensions, government salaries, and interest on the debt. Different levels of government spend varying amounts in each of these areas; for example, defense is primarily a federal government expenditure, while education is more of a local government expenditure. Many state and local expenditures are financed by federal government transfer payments.

The bottom line for business is that many categories of expenditures—particularly defense, health care, education, and transportation—consist of producing capital goods and business and consumer goods and services. As such, business firms are a major beneficiary of government expenditures in these categories. Every day, government agencies at the federal, state, and local level issue RFPs (Requests for Proposals) and solicit bids from the private sector. These might involve building a high school, highway, hospital, or prison; purchasing agricultural goods for hunger relief here or abroad; supporting scientific research and R&D; or launching satellites or building defense machinery, equipment, and materials, among many other activities.

This provides yet another pathway for businesses to seek growth by monitoring government activity and RFPs and learning how to bid successfully for them. Oftentimes, government money includes supporting nongovernment agencies' (NGOs) work. Partnerships can be formed in a few ways—either between government and business or government, business, and an NGO.

Before looking at business opportunities that are available in partnering with government agencies or NGOs, let's note that citizens of different countries have different views about the scale and scope of government in their country. And companies tend to have three views about government's overall impact on business.

One view held by libertarians and right wing conservatives is that while basic government services of safety, national defense, public health, and the administration of justice are necessary, government is primarily a burden and an obstacle to running a business well. Those who hold this view vote for smaller government, lower taxes, and fewer business regulations. One critic of the conservative right asserts that extreme conservatives have proclaimed for many years that "government is bad" and "taxes are evil."[1] Many Americans have bought into this view of government, something that now underlies the extreme polarization of American politics. In his book *Land of Promise*, author Michael Lind observes:

> The founders opposed tyranny. But they advocated self-government, not no government. The Tea Party casts government as inherently oppressive, necessarily wasteful and nearly always damaging to our nation's growth and prosperity. The Republicans see no legitimacy in common goals, which demonize every public enterprise—from public schools to Social Security.[2]

A second view held by moderate conservatives is to use government for passing legislation that provides a social safety net for the poor and welcomes industry interests to lobby for subsidies and tax advantage, under a light regulatory regime. This view supports a moderate level of taxation for a broader scale of government activity. This view favors the freedom of business to lobby local, state, or national government for deregulation or regulatory relief to reduce the cost of doing business and increase the scope and scale of business activity, as well as for trade agreements to open new markets for their goods and services. Moderate conservatives may work through their companies, trade associations, or individually.

The downside of business freedom to interact with government is the ubiquitous practice of corruption, despite all efforts to curb it. Here's a typical scenario: a local developer gives donations to local politicians and wins public sector construction contracts. The developer then gets loans from the local bank on extremely generous terms, thanks to the local politicians. In this way, corruption clearly grows from relations between certain companies and local politicians whom they favor.

A third view is that government should take a proactive role in subsidizing new industries and stimulating economic activity in a down cycle. This goes beyond the typical role of government bond financing to build schools, highways, railways, airports, dams, and needed infrastructure, and instead claims that government should directly contribute to business and economic development.

Infrastructure is typically built by private enterprise in partnership with government through different models of investment-sharing and revenue-sharing. Different countries have used various models, depending on the industry. For example, take the case of railroad development:

- The German government took the lead in building a first-class railway system that is very efficient and high speed in connecting German cities.

- The Spanish government took the lead to make every part of Spain available by rail; however, their system lacked the German level of efficiency and suffered from many cost overruns. Instead of building north–south and separate east–west lines, Spain ended up with many little-used lines. Today it either has to abandon its losing lines or raise ticket prices high enough to cover the costs.

- The U.S. railway system was developed largely by private enterprise companies that raised pools of money from the capital markets, sweetened by public grants. The Vanderbilt family and other railroad barons built or acquired many lines suffering from different standards and difficulties with connections, and U.S. trains generally operated with low speeds. Passenger rail was eventually transferred to government and operates nationally as Amtrak. Additionally, there are many publicly owned commuter lines. Freight rail remains largely in private hands.

- The current Chinese government has the longest public high-speed rail system in the world. By the year 2015, it will extend to 15,000 kilometers, connecting major cities and distant regions of China. It is also lending vast sums to African countries to build government-owned rail systems. The money spent building railroads allows the country to hire many more workers, who will then spend their incomes to generate further economic growth.

Most companies hold all three views of government—getting angry at government at times, exploiting political connections at other times, and partnering with government at still other times to accomplish something. It is hard to generalize about whether economic progress is accelerated when government participates in the development of national growth and infrastructure. California grew to be the ninth-largest economy in the world when taxes were higher and the state's government spent money liberally in improving education and building highways and freeways. Taxes were high—but income growth was higher. Then California voters opted to pass a cap on property taxes. This move, coupled with the recent economic downturn, reduced state and local tax revenues. Now California faces enormous operating and pension costs; the state is being forced to cut its education, social, and health service budgets, and reduce infrastructure maintenance. Several large municipalities, like San Bernardino, have declared bankruptcy. Some of the deterioration of California's quality of life is due to capping taxes that the state badly needed to maintain and improve quality.

Here are the questions that we would like to examine in this chapter:

1. What roles can government play that are good for business and the economy?

2. How can businesses work better with government and NGOs?

3. When does government become more of a damper than an accelerator of economic growth?

4. How can national governments collaborate better for mutual benefit?

What Roles Can Government Play That Are Good for Business and for the Economy?

There is a long history of debate about the size and role of government in general, and the government's role in the economy in particular. This debate is likely to continue forever, with one side prevailing for a while and then the other side gaining support. Yet we can make a strong case for the public and private sectors to operate more collaboratively in today's competitive and interdependent world economy. There are many positive roles that government can play to strengthen the private sector through public investments in R&D and tax incentives for business start-ups and expansion. Correspondingly, there are public sectors that can operate more efficiently by part or full privatization.

Next, we distinguish six roles where government can make a solid contribution to improving the performance of the private sector. They are the government's role in infrastructure, defense, education, safety and health, emergencies, and economic direction.

Infrastructure Roles   Although anyone can start a business, it probably won't go far unless the government or private sector make certain investments in infrastructure. In other words, it is not enough to simply build a restaurant; the restaurant will need electricity, running water, waste disposal, streets and pavements, and other facilitating factors. Private utility companies can supply some of it, but others have to be supplied by government. Citizens expect the government to build streets, roads, bridges, sewage systems, airports, and ports because the private sector lacks the money to build them or cannot charge politically acceptable user fees to make a profit from such facilities.

Foreign investment in infrastructure construction and management can be politically sensitive for national security reason. For example, the 2006 attempted sale of port management business in six major U.S. seaports by British-owned P&O to DP World, a company based in the United Arab Emirates (UAE), caused strong Congressional opposition and was eventually blocked, even though it had White House approval.

State and local governments often work with private investors to Build, Operate, and Transfer (BOT) roads. They grant private rights to operate the roads with tolls at a regulated rate for a period of years, until the road ownership is transferred back to government. We have even seen local governments nowadays sell back public property to the private sector in order to raise enough money to cover current government operating and debt costs. For example, the city of Chicago decided to sell the city-owned parking meters to a private firm for a lump sum payment that represented the present value of the future income stream going to the private sector buyer.

There isn't much controversy surrounding the government's infrastructure responsibilities. Business complaints usually occur when the roads are not maintained, there are an insufficient number of roads or high traffic congestion, or waste removal has slowed down and caused a health hazard.

In the United States, the major difficulty in adding or improving infrastructure is that state and local agencies—for schools, bridges, roads, urban transit—is that voters must approve bond issues for the infrastructure. And they often vote no because the financing increases their property taxes. They consistently vote against school bond issues because most voters do not have children in school. The same can be said for bridges because most voters do not use the same bridge. This is why it usually takes leadership and persuasion to get bond issues through.

Defense Roles   An equally uncontroversial debate surrounds the role of government in protecting its citizens against civil violence or foreign powers who might wage war. Every country will hire police and firemen, and maintain an army, navy and air force to protect the lives and property of its citizens. We hope that most of the time the armed services will be idle and their cost borne by grateful citizens. But there are always military goods makers who lobby Congress for more defense expenditures. The lobbyists argue that defense is undersized and insufficiently funded to support newer and more modern weapon, installations, and equipment. If the lobbyists are successful, Congress concurs and more of the nation's resources will go to support the defense industry. Government costs rise and lead to higher taxes and deeper deficits—which, ironically, the very folks who push for more defense spending then resist.

The lobbyists also publicize national security threats about terrorists, jihadists, and other scourges that will befall the country if we don't move to root them out. Rather than just defend our shores, these lobbyists want us to assert our power in other parts of the world to defend our *interests*. This perspective appeals to patriots, and we end up extending our military presence beyond what may be necessary. However, this approach is good for certain businesses.

Still, some sane voices will claim we have mothballed so many planes, ships, and tanks so much that we really don't need a new type of fighter plane or additional aircraft carriers. What's more, the military leaders occasionally don't even *want* them. But they will be built anyway so that politicians in our 50 states can preserve defense-related jobs in their districts and please the requisite businesses and voters. Unfortunately, people ignore the fact that the large supply of military goods becomes its own excuse for aggressive actions. And since war leads to the destruction of these goods—and therefore the need to replace them—this approach ensures the continuation of employment in military industries.

Education Roles   Citizens broadly accept the view that government needs to supply education—at least at the elementary, high school, community college, and state university level—if the country is to improve its human capital. The private sector cannot supply it, because their charges would be too high and too many citizens wouldn't have the money to pay for it—therefore resulting in fewer educated individuals. So it falls to government to set up public education and citizens to pay for "free" primary education through taxes and through tuition fees at higher levels of education that are moderate compared to private higher education institutions.

However, some parents still opt to send their children to private schools that can charge enough for superior teaching and/or for a religious education. And the worse that public education becomes, the more parents decide to send their children to private schools. For example, Washington, D.C.'s public school system is so bad that hardly anyone in senior levels of the federal government who are living in Washington, D.C. sends their children to public schools. Eminent economist Milton Friedman argued in the 1950s that parents should receive public vouchers to send their children to any school of their choice, which would stimulate competition among schools and raise the quality of public education.[3] Important advances have been made in the charter school movement that imbeds competition within the public education system.

The question remains about the provision of higher education and who should bear the cost. Technically a nation benefits from encouraging as many citizens as possible to get a four-year college degree. In countries such as France and Germany, a college education is free or at least low cost. But as many people know, a four-year college education is very expensive in the United States—even when provided by public state universities such as the University of Michigan, Wisconsin, Illinois, and so on. Those who cannot afford the tuition can go to community colleges at an affordable cost, or skip college altogether. Many people agree by now that the escalation of college costs will have to stop somehow; otherwise, the nation will lose out in its human capital. Germany provides a dual education system enabling students to choose the option of a vocational instead of professional high school education. An apprenticeship with a company is incorporated in the vocational option. The vocational students graduate with several years of experience in a company and are already positioned in the work force when they graduate.

It is clear that business gains from the degree to which the government develops and supports a good education system that produces citizens with quality training and skills. Business also gains by participating in a range of educational projects including school construction and maintenance; developing and selling educational materials; providing classroom supplies; and supplying the heat, lighting, air conditioning, and water systems that schools need to operate.

Safety and Health Roles   Most people want government at the local, state, and federal level to oversee its citizens' safety and health concerns. The United States has established agencies such as the U.S. Department of Agriculture, Department of Health and Human Services, the Federal Drug Administration (FDA), the Centers for Disease Control and Prevention, and other agencies responsible for inspecting food and drug safety. Many of these were established as a result of early scandals in the meat-packing industry and shoddy or dangerous products claiming health and other benefits.

If the government were to provide absolute levels of protection, there would be so many things to watch and evaluate that the public probably would rebel. These agencies are subject to tight budgetary control and often have to focus solely on the most critical health and safety issues. Taxpayers want government to protect health and safety—but only to a certain limit.

Businesses should of course support government regulations that insure safety and health. Good competitors and entire industries suffer when a company produces fake or harmful drugs, food products that contain harmful ingredients, and toys that can harm or poison children.

Emergency Roles   All countries are subject to natural disasters such as hurricanes, floods, or earthquakes—terrible events that kill people and leave the survivors devastated with the loss of their homes and possessions. Most citizens expect their countries to make provisions for emergency aid in the case of natural disasters, whether it be Hurricane Katrina in the United States, the Sichuan earthquake in China, or the Japanese tsunami of 2011. Businesses can help in emergencies with material supplies for rebuilding, food and water supplies, and emergency health care and drug supplies. Individuals and NGOs help with volunteers, monetary contributions, clothing, and a host of emergency services. They also profit from repair. The SPDR S&P Oil & Gas Equipment & Services ETF follows a basket of 27 different firms related to repairing, constructing, and servicing the oil and gas industry. This fund was up 20 percent in 2010 and a good deal of this came from repair sales after Katrina.

Directive Roles   The most controversial role that government can play is to try to direct the economy to move in certain directions. Free marketers want government not to play favorites or influence which industries and companies should grow. They want market forces, not government edicts or money, to influence economic growth. At the same time, many of them also lobby for favors from government to support their industry or company.

Another group favors "guided economic development." They want the government to figure out which industries are needed that will provide the country with good economic growth and a sufficient number of jobs. They will want to identify the industries that are likely to grow more in the future, and to encourage government support for these growth candidates. Government may be willing to subsidize new emerging industries that have great future promise and are environmentally protective. For instance, the United States, as well as other countries, subsidize renewable energy industries in solar and wind power.

The other question inherent in this approach is what government should do about mature industries that have a competitive disadvantage in global trade. They can be left to their slow death, or offered tariff protection and public research and development investment. An example of this is the U.S. government protecting its essential tire and steel industries from foreign low-price competitors by imposing duties allowable under the World Trade Agreement. Some of these actions are upheld by WTO.

Countries such as China, Japan, South Korea, and France are very comfortable guiding their nation's economic development. Just consider how rapidly Japan recovered after World War II by directing development of automobiles, motorcycle, and electronics, and how South Korea chose similar industries to grow. There is always the danger of choosing the wrong industries. But if a government works with business to bet on several new industries, hopefully one or more of them will be successful enough to cover any mistaken choices.

Most businesses are organized into trade and professional associations that work hard to influence government economic policy, even in a "free market" environment. Industries such as solar power in the United States advocate for subsidies, special tax benefits, or duty protection to carry on their work. Companies and different government agencies file thousands of antidumping claims every year. It is hard to imagine companies that are *not* trying to improve their situation through government influence or actions.

In the face of increased global competition, governments are likely to play a growing role in helping domestic companies improve their global competitiveness through commercial support services, R&D funding, tax advantages, strategic trade agreements, and the advocacy of fair trade practices.

How Can Businesses Work Better with Government and NGOs?

Governments around the world tend to be very involved with certain industries that are in the national interest. We have already mentioned the role of governments in helping build a *defense industry* by ordering planes, ships, and munitions. Governments also get involved in *agriculture* in an effort to improve farm products and productivity. The U.S. Department of Agriculture Extension Service has played a major role in helping farmers to use their land more productively and to learn what to grow. The government even pays some farmers to keep their land fallow, either to regain nutrients or to prevent overproduction. Another area of government involvement is supporting the development of high tech industries—robotics, artificial intelligence, biotechnology, energy science, information technology—so that these industries can create more jobs. The United States leads the world in publicly financed scientific research institutions.

In the past, the government had two alternatives when it needed public works (e.g., roads, ports, railroads): either complete the project itself as in the case of TVA and the Army Corps of Engineers, or use procurement procedures and award it to the most attractive bidder. In the latter case, the government often supplied the capital, and the chosen company supplied the labor and materials. When completed, the government or the company may share maintenance and management operations.

We are now hearing more about a third way called *Public-Private Partnerships (PPP)*. These describe cases where the government partners with one or more firms in the private sector. The government or the private sector might propose this partnership and then work out terms on who would supply the capital, labor, and materials, and how to share the project's revenue. The idea behind this approach is to have the private sector bring efficiency, creativity, and some capital, and for the government to also supply capital, assets, land, tax breaks, or guaranteed annual revenues. The private sector firms would typically form a consortium to develop, build, maintain, and operate the project for the contracted period. In some cases, the government would take a revenue stake in the project. Usually there would be agreement between government and the business firms on how to share the risks if things go wrong.

PPPs are especially desirable in a time of low economic growth when government lacks the capital funds to do the project without the private sector's help. The private sector also benefits, since it can propose infrastructure projects to the government and show how it can help fund and develop and operate these projects. So your business-to-business (B2B) firm can seek a new pathway to growth by convincing local, state, or the federal government that the company can supply needed public works through public-private partnerships.

The main PPP projects have to do with creating or improving infrastructure (highways, ports, airports, urban rapid transit, bridges, etc.) and even developing tax-generating real estate (shopping centers and housing development) around these projects. PPPs have been behind some major projects in the past, such as the Channel Tunnel Rail Link between France and the UK; the Beiras Litoral and Alta Shadow Toll Road in Portugal; the M5 tolled motorway in Hungary; the Perpignan-Figueiras Rail Concession, which provided a cross-border link between France and Spain; and Bulgaria's Trakia Motorway Project.[4] Not all of these projects were successful, and public-private partnerships have drawn some criticism about overruns. The biggest concern is about collusion between politicians and politically preferred firms resulting in projects that don't meet expectations.

One thing that is clear is that various countries are in a globalization race. And given the condition of low economic growth, governments can play a positive role in helping companies in a nation improve their competitiveness.

We should say a word here about companies looking for growth opportunities in the area of nongovernment agencies (NGOs). NGOs include nonprofit hospitals, private schools and colleges, private social service organizations, charitable organizations, museums, performing art organizations, environmental organizations, religious institutions, and many other types of organizations that operate on a nonprofit and tax-deductible-contribution basis. These organizations need supplies, physical facilities and equipment, distributors and media—and they pay for these services with money that they raise from their development programs. They run campaigns and solicit support from businesses and government. Some of their budget comes from applying for and winning government grants.

Many NGOs derive substantial revenues for retail stores, licensing merchandise, restaurants, and other commercial activities. For instance, The Metropolitan Museum of Art earned revenues of $95 million for commercial activities and netted almost $6 million in 2011. Museums have to be careful in managing for-profit subsidiaries for commercial revenue. Commercial revenues exceeding 15–30 percent of total museum revenues can threaten their tax-exempt status.

A company seeking growth must pay attention to the needs of the NGO world. A hospital, university, museum, theatre, or religious organization might be planning to expand its building or add a new one, and might already have the funds. Institutional architecture and construction is a big business. Architects and construction companies need to know about these projects and enter the bidding process. A company that gets a good reputation for specializing in one or two areas will have a better chance of winning the bid in these areas. For example, architect Frank Gehry of Gehry Partners, LLP has an incomparable reputation for building new and dazzling museums. He usually can win the bid if the museum can afford his higher price. Another example is Perkins+Will, the top hospital architectural firm in the world.

When Does Government Become More of a Damper than an Accelerator of Economic Growth?

As much as people agree that government should provide most of the six functions mentioned earlier, businesses and their associations will likely always complain that government is dampening rather than accelerating economic activity. Their criticisms fall into three categories.

Regulations   In its efforts to protect the health and safety of its citizens, governments typically require compliance from companies along the lines of "thou shalt not pollute, sell bad meat or fish . . . to citizens." Businesses have to master the guidelines, fill in forms and reports, and generally spend money just to keep up with these regulations. One of the biggest burdens came with the 2002 Sarbanes-Oxley Act, which required a great deal of paperwork and made it the CEO-level's responsibility when unethical behavior occurred somewhere in the company. This and similar regulatory measures certainly contribute to the rapid growth of accounting and legal businesses—but come at the expense of slowing down many companies' growth and profitability.

The issue is one of measuring the benefit versus the cost of a particular regulation before passing it. How necessary is the regulation? How much abuse will it curb? How much time will it consume to understand and comply? How many will comply with it? Will it throttle or aid economic growth? Ideally, we want a regulation's benefit to outweigh its cost.

While overregulation is bad and hurts growth, some regulations are clearly necessary to insure food quality, water and air quality, and prescription drug quality. As someone commented, we don't want to be breathing polluted air, drinking poisoned water, eating toxic food, driving unsafe cars on unsafe tires over unsafe roads, or living in hazardous buildings.

Higher Taxes   A second complaint is that government regulations and regulators have to be paid for by raising taxes on the citizens. There is no such thing as a "no cost regulation"; so the question becomes whether the regulations are efficient and efficiently implemented. At least this will keep the taxpayers' burden down.

Cost of Uncertainty   The legislative process itself involves competing parties engaged in policy setting. Many issues will drag on for months and years, cause a lot of uncertainty, and keep businesses from investing and moving forward. The fact that the Euro, Greece, and Spain's future are all at risk today retards investments by raising interest rates to borrowers. High borrowing costs inhibit state and municipal government bond financing in many U.S. jurisdictions. Many U.S. municipalities and the State of Illinois face very high bond issue costs. Two California cities, Stockton and San Bernardino, have declared bankruptcy. Illinois faces prohibitive bond issue costs. In the United States, the issue of whether the government will continue to raise its spending limit and how to manage harrowing government pension and health costs adds a cloud of uncertainty and retards investment and spending.

How Can National Governments Collaborate Better for Mutual Benefit?

The main danger in a low growth economy is that some nations will concede to the pressure of private sector interests to provide protection by establishing tariff barriers. When such a process of beggar their neighbors begins, each country feels justified in erecting its barriers in self-defense with the unwholesome effect of reducing world trade and business growth. This is similar to the *paradox of thrift* situation in which the effect is reduced growth if each person decides to save more and spend less.

We therefore need the nations of the world to work together through the WTO and other international organizations to facilitate, not restrict, international trade. We need closer coordination between national governments and private sector actors to develop global standardization of commercial rules regarding intellectual property protection, trade governance, shipping and transportation regulations, banking and finance regulations, and communication and Internet standards.

Free Trade is not the only issue for global economic growth and consequent business growth. We have international financial institutions like the IMF that pull capital from developed nations to help less developed economies that are financially distressed. We are at an epochal moment as we follow the complex and tenuous efforts of the European Central Bank (ECB) and Euro stabilization mechanisms to work with its southern tier distressed economies to sustain the Euro and revive economic and business growth in Europe.

Conclusion

Government and its agencies play an important role in every country. At a minimum, a government may limit itself to defense, infrastructure, and education. Even in these few roles, government needs to have businesses help carry out projects by providing goods and services such as military equipment and supplies, rail, seaports and airports, highways, schools, and other projects. In some countries, government takes on many additional roles that involve spending public money on needed goods and services. In these efforts, governments typically invite for-profit companies to submit bids for the work to be done. Today, governments are turning increasingly to Public-Private Partnerships (PPPs) to secure capital for infrastructure development. It is also the case that nongovernment agencies (NGOs) will need additional goods and services. Although companies have to fill out many forms when bidding for government and NGO work, many of these jobs can be profitable—especially to companies who have wide and deep experience working with government and NGOs. When total business and consumer spending declines in an economy, companies should remember that governments of countries with a strong economy can increase their spending—something that will provide companies with growth opportunities.

Questions

1. List any work that your company has done for government agencies. Has it generally been profitable or unprofitable? If it has been unprofitable, why?

2. Can you identify any government work that would be profitable for your company to pursue today? Do you have a good shot at winning the bid and making an adequate profit?

3. Have you served any particular sector of the NGO world and developed expertise and a reputation in that sector? What is keeping you from intensifying your effort in this sector?

4. Is your company losing sales in a foreign country that has erected higher tariff or nontariff barriers? Are you lobbying your government to raise tariff and nontariff barriers against that country? Is this the best response to the problem?

EPILOGUE

We are currently living in the most perilous times since the Great Depression. And the peril now, as it was then, is global. A large number of forces—recession and high unemployment, decaying infrastructure, poverty, military and religious conflicts, environmental concerns, political polarization—have converged to paralyze action. And the various affected actors—individuals, communities, businesses, governments, political leaders, science and technology, social and cultural institutions, and NGOs—must act in new ways to save their own sphere, and the global sphere as well. In short, we *all* have to do our part to get the world economy growing again.

This book is about one very important sphere—business. Business has to grow and cooperate with the other spheres to do this. Business has to tap into its dynamic source of growth—which has always been and will always be the customer. There is plenty of wealth in the world, but the wealth, however unbalanced its distribution, is not being spent or invested. The latch to open the door of economic growth has always been consumption, whether it involves domestic or international trade. And the key to kick-starting consumption lies in the power and application of marketing.

In perilous times, people reduce their consumption and save. They fear the future and want to save for rainy days ahead. This is what is currently taking place in the United States, China,

Europe, and all over the world. And when people don't spend on consumption, industries don't spend on investment. Saving can be good for an individual; however, it is usually bad for a whole society. Consumers and businesses need to understand the *paradox of thrift*. If everyone saves more and spends less, companies will earn less, and companies will cut their costs and jobs. This paradox says that a high rate of saving during a recession makes people ultimately poorer.

There is always a great deal of spending and investing during good times. The challenge during good times is to keep individuals, businesses, and governments from spending too much—to prevent them from going beyond their income, net revenues, and reasonable limits of credit. Indeed, these are the actions that brought us to the present mess. But our times are different now. We are deleveraging *too* much and must start to spend again.

Marketing's job has always been to get the ball rolling on spending. And it's not about spending for spending's sake, or building idle pyramids. We are talking about spending and investing to meet the vast unsatisfied needs of billions of people on the planet. We have not yet come to a "no-need" world society.

And we can only do this by utilizing marketing to mobilize those with money to invest and spend for growth. Naturally, we need monetary, fiscal, and trade policy; however, these should not be the dog that wags marketing's tail. In contrast, marketing should wag the tail of economic policy. Things have to be turned upside down. It is companies, entrepreneurs, and consumers who must beckon support of government and politicians; not the other way around. To get marketing rolling, businesses, entrepreneurs, and consumers have to influence the government to support market activity. The extreme positions that political parties are taking on the two alternative remedies—austerity vs. stimulus spending—are hampering economic recovery. The truth is we can apply *both* in a balanced way, as evidenced by this Exhibit.

The Debate between Austerity and Stimulus Spending as Economic Recovery Solutions

The United States has experienced a recession almost every five years. There seems to be something in the nature of free enterprise capitalism that produces these recessions. Reading Karl Marx's *Das Capital* has become fashionable again in some circles—not because of the book's political analysis, but because of its economic analysis. Marx observed that as an economy grows, speculation also grows because of the assumption that growth will continue. It reaches a point where a bubble grows and then bursts, and the boom turns into a bust. Wages don't grow enough during the growth period and there isn't enough widespread purchasing power to keep high spending going. Marx put the problem as one of the immiseration of the working class not having the money to buy the products that they produce.[1]

Of course, the dynamics are more complex in real life. However, it is true that wealth has tended to get more concentrated in the United States and many other countries. The estimate is that the top 1 percent of the richest people control 43 percent of the wealth in the United States today, and account for 24 percent of the income earned. And the top 10 percent are experiencing a substantially higher income percentage growth than the 90 percent who have not experienced income growth in real terms. The result is more wealth concentration than ever before, which ironically means that the rich themselves will end the cycle of growth. Consumer spending has historically accounted for 70 percent of the GDP. However, it is getting harder for consumers to keep up this spending level in the face of mortgage defaults, tight lending, limited credit, and high unemployment.

On the policy front, there are two broad and diametrically opposed answers given as to how to cure the economic malaise: namely, a government policy of austerity versus a government policy of stimulus spending.

Austerity as the Solution. Those who advocate practicing austerity say the problem is that the government has grown too large and is spending wastefully on entitlement programs such as Social Security, Medicare and Medicaid, college loans, and disability programs, and that this spending should be reduced or eliminated. They fail to assign blame to the government's huge military expenditures, and they oppose new taxes to pay for these programs. The cuts that they recommend for government mean fewer teachers, police, and firemen, as if most public employees are political hacks or should be in the private sector. They don't bother to mention the fact that the private sector doesn't have jobs to absorb these government workers. What's worse is that they take no account of the fact that when these government employees lose their jobs and don't find employment, they go on unemployment insurance and tighten their belts—making even fewer dollars available to be spent to prop up consumer spending. In fact, one could argue that the very adoption of austerity is the major cause of increased unemployment. Austerity causes everyone to tighten their belts, which results in insufficient demand for products and therefore for jobs. An increasing number of economists have attributed Western Europe's worsening situation to the imposition of strict austerity measures pushed on Europe by Germany.

Austerity advocates are extremely concerned about the debt burden and of avoiding defaults and inflation. They act as if defaults and inflation are just around the corner, rather than outcomes that might take place in 5 or 10 years. They don't want the debt to increase further, and they object to the government borrowing or printing more money. As far as they're concerned, this will cause inflation and devalue the dollar, thus hurting the creditors. They want debt to be borne by the debtors, not the creditors. Thus, when a family can't continue to make mortgage payments because their home is under water, austerity advocates want the bank to foreclose—thereby causing the debtor instead of the bank to suffer, even when the bank was overly liberal in lending money to people who took out large mortgages to buy their home. The austerity issue is really a question of who pays the bill—how much of the loss is born by debtors and how much by creditors.

The other argument austerity theorists make is that businesses need a greater incentive to invest. One source would be lower business and personal taxes so that businesses and individuals would have more money and incentive to invest. Of course, this assumes that demand and spending would be large enough to invite investment opportunities. There seems to be a mismatch between supply side economics which says that sellers are the key to investment and demand side economics which says that buyers must have enough purchasing power to buy.

Stimulus Spending as the Solution. The contrary solution is to advocate another round of stimulus spending. Liberal economists advocate for this, most notably Paul Krugman, who has argued that the first stimulus round in 2008–2009 was too little—while austerity advocates charge that the first stimulus round was a failure. It wasn't spent on infrastructure, but went largely to state and local governments to maintain their public employees. The counterargument, however, is that the stimulus spending did have a positive impact on the economy. Without the stimulus money, many states would have laid off more state employees and U.S. unemployment could have risen from 8.3 to 11 or 12 percent—not to mention all the additional unemployment payments that governments would have to make.[2]

The argument for moving to a second round of stimulus spending as soon as possible is based on two points. First, the most urgent problem facing the U.S. economy is unemployment, not a U.S. default. The government can print money to pay its bills. So let's create jobs now, as this will lead to a needed increase in business and government revenue. Short-term bond yields are likely to remain stable and manageable, so long as the U.S. dollar remains a safe haven reserve currency. The Chinese Yuan is a long way from challenging this, although it is now finding acceptance in trade clearance in S.E. Asia, Russia, Brazil, and elsewhere. And the charge that this would create an inflationary spiral is highly unlikely, because all the forces point to deflation rather than inflation. It is in the nature of a highly competitive economy where companies are struggling to survive that they will cut costs and prices, rather than raise prices. Inflation only occurs when prices are raised rapidly. So the argument is that another round of stimulus spending to create new jobs is unlikely to increase the chances of a runaway inflation.

If both sides would accept the primacy of job creation now rather than reducing the debt burden, then everyone could begin to take steps toward recovery. They should also realize and accept the fact that the major area of job creation lies with our decaying infrastructure—the various bridges, roads, rail, and other infrastructure that need repair, maintenance, and greater productivity. All of this requires construction work and the reemployment of the many persons in the construction industry who have been without work since the housing bust in 2008. Once we begin to spend money on infrastructure improvement, it revives such industries as steel, cement, and other material industries as well as increasing the need for additional equipment and services. Hopefully, creating new jobs will have a ripple effect and get enough other industries to raise their spending—potentially improving consumer confidence enough to increase consumer spending.

Is resolution possible between the two polemical positions of austerity versus stimulus? We contrasted the extreme positions of both sides as if no moderate position exists. Can't we say that there is a spectrum of opinions between both extremes and refer to the moderate position of the Simpson-Bowles Report, which calls for a mix of debt reduction and increased taxes?[3] Though it was not legislated for partisan reasons, it is a moderate point of reference with wide political support, especially among independent voters who are 30 percent of the U.S. electorate.

Once the two sides agree to a moderate position, much of the political bickering and economic uncertainty that plagues business and deters investment and lending will clear up and happy times may come again.

We need spending and investment to build better roads, telecommunications, energy systems, water sanitation and conservation systems, and other infrastructure. There is no shortage of capital; there is simply a lack of confidence and cooperation. Simply put, we need individuals, businesses, organizations, and governments to spend more. The science and practice of marketing must combat the fear of spending and resist the impulse of fearful saving. Marketing must play a stronger role in generating confidence and hope in the future. Marketing has the unique capacity to sell the dream of a better life for all.

We need businesses to create more products, services, and experiences at irresistible prices. We need more new iPads and fewer financial derivatives. We need to restore a *production and marketing culture* and reduce the *money culture* wherein people try to make money by manipulating money. We need to bring in the Marketers, the New Economists, to inspire consumers to buy and companies to invest in exciting things. Economists don't know much about marketing because they like abstractions, whereas marketers like to deal with the real-world dynamics of consumption, competition, and innovation. We propose that both marketing and classical economists would gain substantially if they worked closer together in influencing public policy as well as company strategy.

Every company needs two marketing departments, not one. The normal marketing department is tactical; its job is to sell the goods that the company currently produces. It uses product, price, place, and promotion—the famous 4Ps—to do the job. It brings its offerings to existing market channels and creates new channels to carry its offerings. It uses traditional media to broadcast its messages, and is now using digital databases and social media to more finely deliver the right message at the right time to the right person.

The other marketing department is strategic. It is not involved in moving today's goods but in preparing tomorrow's offerings. Companies need to think about what their customers will want and expect three years from now, and companies must anticipate their future competitors. They must imagine the new technology and media that may become available. They must embody an innovative mind-set to visualize the opportunities being released by advancing technology and globalization. They need to feed top management a continuous blast of new ideas.

Growth is possible in these dismal times. We opened our book with a description of Nine Major Megatrends, all of which create opportunities. Then we pointed out Eight Pathways to Growth. Some companies pursue only one pathway and miss seeing the opportunities that the other seven offer. Other companies may be dipping into several pathways but performing on a very average level. We wrote this book with descriptions and prescriptions on how to grow your business. We included questions so that your company can see how it stands on the different pathways to growth.

Marketers are trained to recognize opportunities. They are conditioned to see opportunities in every crisis. We hope that companies can turn from thinking crisis to thinking about how marketing can be used to identify new opportunities for growth.

NOTES

Introduction

1.   "Negative Population Growth: Historical and Future Trends," www.npg.org/popfacts.htm.

2.   Thomas B. Edsall, "The Hollowing Out," *New York Times*, July 8, 2012.

3.   Rana Foroohar, "Slowdown Goes Global," *Time*, June 18, 2012, p. 43.

4.   Mark Penn and E. Kinney Zalesne, *Microtrends: The Small Forces behind Tomorrow's Big Changes* (New York: Twelve, 2007).

5.   Greg Verdino, *Micromarketing: Get Big Results by Thinking and Acting Small* (New York: McGraw-Hill, 2010).

Chapter 1

1.   Jack Neff, "P&G Plots Growth Path through Services," *Advertising Age*, March 22, 2010.

2.   See Tim Calkins, *Defend Your Brand: How Smart Companies Use Defensive Strategy to Deal with Competitive Attacks* (New York: Palgrave Macmillan, 2012).

3.   Kotler Marketing Group, *Marketing Through Difficult Times: Best Practices of Companies that Found Ways to Prosper During the Great Recession, 2011* (Washington, DC: Tony Kotler, 2011).

4.   Philip Kotler, "Phasing Out Weak Products," *Harvard Business Review* 43, no. 2 (March–April 1965): 107–118.

Chapter 2

1.   Christine Birkner, "10 Minutes with John Goodman," *Marketing News*, October 30, 2011, 28–32.

2. Mark J. Penn and E. Kinney Zalesne, *Microtrends: The Small Forces Behind Tomorrow's Big Changes* (New York: Twelve, Hachette Book Group, 2007).

3. *Mitchells Offers the Perfect One to One Fit*, FBNews.net/Smartbiz.com.

4. Stacy Straczynski, "Probing the Minds of Teenage Consumers," *AdWeek*, September 23, 2009.

5. Hermann Simon, *Hidden Champions: Lessons from 500 of the World's Best Unknown Companies* (Boston: Harvard Business School Press, 1996).

6. Theodore Levitt, "Marketing Myopia," *Harvard Business Review* (July-August 1960).

7. Euclid Industrial Maintenance and Cleaning, FBNews.net/Smartbiz .com.

8. Frederick Reichheld, "One Number You Need to Grow," *Harvard Business Review* (December 2003).

9. James L. Heskett, W. Earl Sasser, and Joe Wheeler, *The Ownership Quotient: Putting the Service Profit Chain to Work for Unbeatable Competitive Advantage* (Boston: Harvard Business Press, 2008).

10. Ben McConnell, Jackie Huba, and Guy Kawasaki, *Creating Customer Evangelists* (Washington, DC, Kaplan Publishing); Matthew W. Ragas and Bolivar J. Bueno, *The Power of Cult Branding* (Roseville, CA: Prima Venture, 2002); and Ken Blanchard and Sheldon Bowles, *Creating Raving Fans*, (New York: Morrow, 1993).

11. Birkner, "10 Minutes with John Goodman," 30.

12. Ibid.

13. See Michael Lowenstein, "Employee Ambassadorship," Harris Interactive, 2007.

14. http://money.cnn.com/magazines/fortune/best-companies/2012/ full_list.

Chapter 3

1. www.interbrand.com/best-global-brands.

2. For more on sensory marketing, see Martin Lindstrom, *Brand Sense: Sensory Secrets Behind the Stuff We Buy* (New York: Free Press, 2005).

3. See Kevin Lane Keller, *Strategic Brand Management: Building, Measuring, and Managing Brand Equity*, 4th ed. (Upper Saddle River, NJ, Prentice-Hall, 2013).

Chapter 4

1. Masahiro Fujita, President of Sony's System Technologies Laboratories, quoted in, Tellis, Gerard J. (2013), *Unrelenting Innovation: How to Create a Culture of Market Dominance* (San Francisco, CA: Jossey-Bass, 2013) January, forthcoming.

2. Some parts of this chapter have appeared in Fernando Trias de Bes and Philip Kotler, *Winning at Innovation: The A-F Method* (New York: Palgrave Macmillan, 2011), with permission.

3. Gilda Waisburd, *Creativity and Innovation*, Extension Forestry Reform, 1287 Col. Bosques de las Lomas CP 11700, Mexico, DF.

4. Trias de Bes and Kotler, *Winning at Innovation*.

5. Steven J. Spear and John Kenagy, Deaconess-Glover Hospital (A), Harvard Business School Case, Prod. #: 601022-PDF-ENG, July 19, 2000.

6. yet2.com Inc., www.businessweek.com/magazine/content/ 06_17/b3981401.htm.

7. Peter C. Honebein and Roy F. Cammarano, "Customers at Work," *Marketing Management* 15, no. 8 (January-February 2006): 26–31; Peter C. Honebein and Roy F. Cammarano, *Creating Do-It-Yourself Customers: How Great Customer Experiences Build Great Companies* (Mason, OH: Texere Southwestern Educational Publishing, 2005).

8. Trias de Bes and Kotler, *Winning at Innovation*.

9. Stephan Thomke and Eric von Hippel, "Customers as Innovators: A New Way to Create Value," *Harvard Business Review* (April 2002): 74–81.

10. Pioneering work in this area is represented by Eric von Hippel, "Lead Users: A Source of Novel Product Concepts," *Management Science* 32, no. 7 (July 1986): 791–805. Also see Eric von Hippel, *Democratizing Innovation* (Cambridge: MIT Press, 2005); and Pamela D. Morrison, John H. Roberts, and David F. Midgley, "The Nature of Lead Users and Measurement of Leading Edge Status," *Research Policy*, 33, no. 2 (2004): 351–362.

11. Jeff Howe, *Crowdsourcing: Why the Power of the Crowd Is Driving the Future of Business* (New York: Crown Business, 2008).

12. See "Fiat Mio, the World's First Crowdsourced Car" http://www.ideaconnection.com/open-innovation-success/Fiat-Mio-the-World's-First-Crowdsourced-Car-00273.html.

13. Guido Jouret, "Inside Cisco's Search for the Next Big Idea," *Harvard Business Review* (September 2009): 43–45; Anya Kamentz, "The Power of the Prize," *Fast Company* (May 2008): 43–45; Cisco. www.cisco.com/web/solutions/iprize/index.html.

14. Patricia Seybold, *Outside Innovation: How Your Customers Will Codesign Your Company's Future* (New York: HarperCollins, 2006).

15. Philip Kotler and Kevin Keller, *Marketing Management*, 13th ed. (Upper Saddle River, NJ: Pearson/Prentice-Hall, 2008), 577.

16. John W. Heinke Jr. and Chun Zhang, "Increasing Supplier-Driven Innovation," *MIT Sloan Management Review* (Winter 2010) 41–46; Eric (Er) Fang, "Customer Participation and the Trade-Off Between New Product Innovativeness and Speed to Market," *Journal of Marketing* 72 (July 2008): 90–104. Note that this research also shows that customer involvement can also slow the development process if a high level of interaction and coordination is required across stages.

17. "Asia's New Model Economy," *The Economist*, October 1, 2011, p. 14.

18. Robert G. Cooper, "Stage-Gate System: A New Tool for Managing New Products," *Business Horizons* (May-June 1990).

19. Trias de Bes and Kotler, *Winning at Innovation*, Chapter 2.

20. Ibid., see Chapter 9.

21. Example extracted from W. Chan Kim and Renee Mauborgne, *Blue Ocean Strategy: How to Create Uncontested Market Space and Make the Competition Irrelevant* (Boston: Harvard Business School Press, 2005).

22. www.innovaforum.com.

23. "The World's Most Innovative Companies. Special Report—Innovation," *Business Week*, April 24, 2006.

24. See Philip Kotler, Hermawan Kartajaya, and David Young, *Attracting Investors: A Marketing Approach to Finding Funds for Your Business* (Hoboken, NJ: John Wiley & Sons, 2004).

25. C. K. Prahalad, *The Innovation Sandbox*, Strategy+Business. Booz Company, reprint #06306.

26. Philip Kotler and Fernando Trias de Bes, *Lateral Marketing: A New Approach to Finding Product, Market, and Marketing Mix Ideas* (Hoboken, NJ: John Wiley & Sons, 2003).

27. Kotler, Kartajaya, and Young, *Attracting Investors*.

Chapter 5

1. "A Profile of U.S. Importing and Exporting Companies, 2009–2010," U.S. Department of Commerce, Washington, D.C. 20230, April 12, 2012.

2. www.census.gov/econ/smallbus.html#.

3. See Tyler Cowen, "What Export-Oriented America Means," *The American Interest* (May-June 2012).

4. See Country Projections in OECD Economic Outlook, www.oecd.org/OECD EconomicOutlook.

Chapter 6

1. Michael E. Porter, "From Competitive Advantage to Corporate Strategy," *Harvard Business Review* (May 1987).

2. "KPMG Identifies Six Key Factors for Successful Mergers and Acquisitions; 83% of Deals Fail to Enhance Shareholder Value," *Risk World*, November 29, 1999.

3. Ulrike Malmendier, Enrico Moretti, and Florian Peters, "Winning by Losing: Evidence on Overbidding in Mergers," April 2011, http://economics.mit.edu/files/6628.

4. See "FTC to Challenge Nestlé, Dreyer's Merger," www.ftc.gov/opa/2003/03/dreyers.shtm.

5. See "Joint Ventures and Strategic Alliances," *Encyclopedia of Business*, 2nd ed. www.referenceforbusiness.com/encyclopedia

6. www.abrakadoodle.com/Crayola.htm.

7. See "Co-branding," *Wikipedia*.

Chapter 7

1. These six corporate initiatives are described in Philip Kotler, David Hessekiel, and Nancy R. Lee, *Good Works! Marketing and Corporate Initiatives That Build a Better World . . . and the Bottom Line* (Hoboken, NJ: John Wiley and Sons, 2012).

Chapter 8

1.   Paul Begala, "Blame the Right: The GOP Puts Party Before Country Every Time," *Newsweek*, May 21, 2012, p. 14.

2.   Michael Lind, *Land of Promise: An Economic History of the United States* (New York: Harper/Harper Collins, 2012). This economic history of the United States argues that the country thrives when the federal government acts as a robust partner to private enterprise.

3.   Milton Friedman, "The Role of Government in Education," in *Economics and the Public Interest*, ed. Robert A. Solo, Rutgers, NJ., Rutgers University Press,1955.

4.   See ADB Institute,"Illustrative Examples of PPP in the EU," www.adbi.org/working-paper/2011/05/13/4531.financial .instruments.ppp.infrastructural.dev.eu/illustrative.examples.of.ppp .in.the.eu/.

Epilogue

1.   See "Marx to Market," *Bloomberg Business Week*, September 19–25, 2011, 10–11.

2.   See Dylan Matthews, "Did the stimulus work? A review of the nine best studies on the subject," *Washington Post*, August 24, 2011. "Of the nine studies I've found, six find that the stimulus had a significant, positive effect on employment and growth, and three find that the effect was either quite small or impossible to detect."

3.   Jeanne Sahadi, "Bowles-Simpson Back on Table," *CNN Money*, April 17, 2012.

INDEX